Basketball Greats

Basketball Greats

Other books in the History Makers series:

History MAKERS

Basketball Greats

By Joanne Mattern

LUCENT BOOKS®

THOMSON

GALE

San Diego • Detroit • New York • San Francisco • Cleveland
New Haven, Conn. • Waterville, Maine • London • Munich

LIBRARY OF CONGRESS CATALOGING-IN-PUBLICATION DATA

Mattern, Joanne, 1963–
    Basketball greats / by Joanne Mattern.
       v.   cm. — (History makers)
Summary: Provides a brief history of the sport of basketball and profiles six players who
changed the sport and, in some cases, society itself as they reached for their dreams.
Includes bibliographical references (p.   ) and index.
Contents: George Mikan, the big man — Wilt Chamberlain, the greatest game of all —
Kareem Abdul-Jabbar, scoring champion — Magic Johnson, making things happen —
John Stockton, a true team player — Michael Jordan, the greatest ever.
    ISBN 1-59018-228-6 (alk. paper)
    1. Basketball players—United States—Biography—Juvenile literature.
[1. Basketball players.] I. Title. II. Series.
    GV884.A1 M37 2003
    796.323909292—dc21

                                                                              2002009140

CONTENTS

FOREWORD

The literary form most often referred to as "multiple biography" was perfected in the first century A.D. by Plutarch, a perceptive and talented moralist and historian who hailed from the small town of Chaeronea in central Greece. His most famous work, *Parallel Lives*, consists of a long series of biographies of noteworthy ancient Greek and Roman statesmen and military leaders. Frequently, Plutarch compares a famous Greek to a famous Roman, pointing out similarities in personality and achievements. These expertly constructed and very readable tracts provided later historians and others, including playwrights like Shakespeare, with priceless information about prominent ancient personages and also inspired new generations of writers to tackle the multiple biography genre.

The Lucent History Makers series proudly carries on the venerable tradition handed down from Plutarch. Each volume in the series consists of a set of five to eight biographies of important and influential historical figures who were linked together by a common factor. In *Rulers of Ancient Rome*, for example, all the figures were generals, consuls, or emperors of either the Roman Republic or Empire; while the subjects of *Fighters Against American Slavery*, though they lived in different places and times, all shared the same goal, namely the eradication of human servitude. Mindful that politicians and military leaders are not (and never have been) the only people who shape the course of history, the editors of the series have also included representatives from a wide range of endeavors, including scientists, artists, writers, philosophers, religious leaders, and sports figures.

Each book is intended to give a range of figures—some well known, others less known; some who made a great impact on history, others who made only a small impact. For instance, by making Columbus's initial voyage possible, Spain's Queen Isabella I, featured in *Women Leaders of Nations*, helped to open up the New World to exploration and exploitation by the European powers. Inarguably, therefore, she made a major contribution to a series of events that had momentous consequences for the entire world. By contrast, Catherine II, the eighteenth-century Russian queen, and Golda Meir, the modern Israeli prime minister, did not play roles of global impact; however, their policies and actions significantly influenced the historical development of both their own countries and their regional neighbors. Regardless of their relative importance in the greater historical scheme, all of the figures chronicled in the History Makers series made contributions to posterity; and their public achievements, as well as what is known about their private lives, are presented and evaluated in light of the most recent scholarship.

In addition, each volume in the series is documented and substantiated by a wide array of primary and secondary source quotations. The primary source quotes enliven the text by presenting eyewitness views of the times and culture in which each history maker lived; while the secondary source quotes, taken from the works of respected modern scholars, offer expert elaboration and/ or critical commentary. Each quote is footnoted, demonstrating to the reader exactly where biographers find their information. The footnotes also provide the reader with the means of conducting additional research. Finally, to further guide and illuminate readers, each volume in the series features photographs, two bibliographies, and a comprehensive index.

The History Makers series provides both students engaged in research and more casual readers with informative, enlightening, and entertaining overviews of individuals from a variety of circumstances, professions, and backgrounds. No doubt all of them, whether loved or hated, benevolent or cruel, constructive or destructive, will remain endlessly fascinating to each new generation seeking to identify the forces that shaped their world.

Big Men of the Game

In 1891, a physical education teacher named Dr. James Naismith wanted to find a new game for his students at the YMCA in Springfield, Massachusetts, to play indoors during the winter. Naismith nailed two wooden peach baskets to the balcony railings, handed his students a leather soccer ball, and told them to toss it into the baskets to score points. The game of basketball was born.

Over the next one hundred years, basketball changed from a game played in college gyms, dance halls, and small arenas to a multibillion-dollar business that is one of the most popular sports in the world. The players have changed, too. At first, they were short men wearing long tights who were not known outside of their hometowns and who made barely enough money to live on. Today, basketball players are flashy, world-famous athletes whose celebrity endorsements sell everything from soft drinks to sneakers.

The style of basketball has changed, too. From a slow-paced game where teams might only score 20 points a game, basketball has evolved into a fast-paced, physically demanding game dominated by very tall men who easily score 20, 30, or more points a night.

As with any sport, basketball has had many outstanding players. However, basketball could not have become the immensely popular game it is today without the contributions of several outstanding men. These players have gone far beyond the elite ranks to achieve greatness. They did so by setting apparently unbreakable records or personally changing the way the game was played.

George Mikan was basketball's first "big man." At first considered clumsy and too tall to be successful, Mikan's height and style made him the dominant player of the late 1940s and 1950s and changed the way the game was played.

Wilt Chamberlain is remembered as an electrifying player. Among his many records is one of the most incredible in all sports: scoring 100 points in a single game.

Dr. James Naismith invented basketball to entertain his YMCA students during the long winters in Massachusetts.

Kareem Abdul-Jabbar was such a dominant player that one of his shots was outlawed by the National Collegiate Athletic Association. He went on to score the most career points in NBA history and become one of the game's most important players.

Magic Johnson was known as a player who could set up plays and make incredible things happen on the court. His achievements on the court were overshadowed by the stunning news that he had contracted HIV, the AIDS virus, but Johnson went on to achieve greatness off the court as well, as an African American business-man and an outspoken advocate of AIDS awareness.

Although many players achieve fame as individuals, others find true greatness as part of a team. John Stockton is a player who is often overlooked, even though his partnership with teammate Karl Malone has helped Stockton to become the career leader in assists and steals—and one of the most respected men in the sport.

And then there is Michael Jordan, who has been called the greatest athlete of all time. He has the highest scoring average in basketball history and dominated the game during the 1990s. Jordan also achieved fame outside of sports, thanks to his many commercial endorsements and appearances. He has become a celebrity whose fame far outshines his incredible basketball career.

Examining the lives and careers of these six special athletes highlights not only the talents that made them such incredible players but the ways they changed the game of basketball and, in some cases, society itself. The stories of these six basketball greats can show us how to achieve our dreams—and sometimes the impossible.

CHAPTER 1

George Mikan: The Big Man

One night in December 1949, the marquee at New York City's Madison Square Garden announced a sporting event in a very unusual way. It read, "George Mikan vs. the Knicks." Actually, the Knicks were playing the Minneapolis Lakers that night. But the Lakers center, George Mikan, was such an amazing player that it really did seem like he could defeat the opposing team all by himself. In fact, Mikan became such a dominant player, he changed the way the game of basketball was played.

A Clumsy Child

George Lawrence Mikan was born on June 18, 1924, in Edina, Minnesota. When he was a child, his family moved to a farm near Joliet, Illinois.

Mikan did not seem to have the makings of a star athlete. Author Brad Herzog commented that as a child, "his biggest athletic accomplishment was winning the county marbles championship."[1] Mikan was so nearsighted that he had to wear thick glasses to see. He was also clumsy, partly because of his height. By the age of eleven, he was already six feet tall. "My height nearly wrecked my life" Mikan later recalled. "I was a freak. I was like the fat lady in the circus or the tattooed man."[2]

Despite his awkwardness, Mikan enjoyed sports. He showed promise as a baseball pitcher, but his real love was playing basketball with other boys in the neighborhood. Often, these games were refereed by Mikan's grandmother.

However, when Mikan tried out for the Joliet Catholic High School basketball team, he was cut because the coach did not think anyone could play while wearing glasses. Discouraged, Mikan transferred to Quigley Prep in Chicago, a Catholic seminary school whose students were interested in studying for the priesthood.

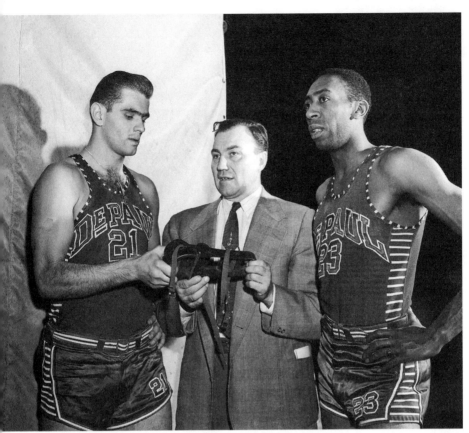

George Mikan's college basketball coach Ray Meyer stands between two of his team's players. He holds an iron shoe he used for training.

A College Star

Although Mikan graduated from Quigley in 1941, he decided he did not want to become a priest after all. Instead, he gave basketball another shot. Mikan tried out for Notre Dame's Coach George Keogan. The tryout did not go well. "They kept throwing the ball at my feet, and I kicked more three-pointers that day than anyone on the football team,"[3] Mikan recalled years later. Keogan kindly told him he would be better off at a smaller, less competitive school.

Around the same time, Mikan was invited to play for Chicago's DePaul University. Mikan accepted the offer and joined DePaul's varsity team in 1942. His coach was a man named Ray Meyer.

During the first half of the twentieth century, few basketball players were more than six feet tall. Basketball historian Robert W. Peterson explains that

Conventional wisdom was that large men were too clumsy and uncoordinated to play basketball. Better a six-footer who was fairly fast, quick, and graceful than a really large man who stumbled over his own feet. No doubt many big men accepted that judgment and never seriously tried to learn the game, or if they did try, faced ridicule for their initial efforts and dropped out.[4]

When he joined DePaul's team, George Mikan was six feet, ten inches tall. He believed the conventional wisdom that big men could not play basketball, because "no matter where a tall guy went in those days, there was always someone to tell him he couldn't do something."[5]

However, Ray Meyer had a different, and revolutionary, idea. His theory was that "big men go to the basket; little guys go away."[6] Meyer worked extensively with Mikan, helping the "big man" to develop his skills. He realized that Mikan was not clumsy. "It was a case of his just growing too fast and not playing much basketball," Meyer later said of Mikan's apparent lack of ability. "He was awkward. What he needed was some agility and finesse."[7]

Mikan spent hours on repetitive drills that helped him to coordinate his arms and legs. "I worked with that kid two to 2½ hours every day," Meyer recalled.

> There was no limit then to the length of workouts. I'd have George take 250 hook shots with his right hand, then 250 more with his left. . . . I had him skip rope like a boxer. I brought in a coed to teach him to dance. I had him go one-on-one with a 5'5" guard, Billy Donato, and that was like watching an elephant guard a fly. I did everything I could to improve his agility because I wanted a big guy like that playing for me. . . . I knew then that a big man could score more points by accident than a little one could trying hard. Oh, George's practices were something to behold. The thing was, he really wanted to be good, so he worked as hard as any player I ever had. And he was so intelligent, he could adjust to anything I gave him. . . . I don't think I ever had more fun than I had that season with George. It was like watching a flower bloom.[8]

Meyer's workouts paid off, especially the drills involving shooting hook shots with either hand. "I had a right-handed hook and everyone had been overplaying me," Mikan recalled years later.

Blocking a shot by an Oklahoma A&M player, Mikan (in white) demonstrates his height and agility.

After completing Meyer's drills, "My lefty hook became better than my right, and it was hard for anyone to stop me."[9]

Mikan also learned to have confidence in his ability. "As soon as George stopped feeling sorry for himself and realized his height was something to be admired, he was on his way to being great,"[10] Meyer said.

Meyer's faith in Mikan's ability soon paid off. By the end of the season, Mikan was scoring an average of 10 points a game. He led DePaul to a 19-5 record and a spot in the National Collegiate Athletic Association (NCAA) tournament. The following year, DePaul was 22-4. The team appeared in the National Invitational Tournament (NIT), which at the time was more prestigious than the NCAA tournament. Mikan was also named to the All-American team.

Changing the Rules

Mikan was so much taller than the other players that he was able to knock the ball away as it was headed to the basket. This was called goaltending, and it was legal in basketball at that time. In

1944, however, the NCAA banned goaltending because Mikan was deflecting so many shots, the other team did not have a chance.

Mikan did not let the prohibition against goaltending slow him down. Instead, he concentrated on scoring. During the 1944–1945 season, he averaged 20.9 points per game, the highest average in college basketball. In the NIT semifinals against Rhode Island State, Mikan scored an incredible 53 points. That was more than the entire Rhode Island team!

During the 1945–1946 season, Mikan averaged more than 23 points per game. For the third straight year, he was named to the All-American team. By the time he graduated from DePaul in 1946, he had scored an impressive total of 1,870 points. Now it was time for new challenges.

The Birth of the NBA

In 1946, Mikan signed a contract with the Chicago American Gears, a professional team in the National Basketball League (NBL). Mikan was paid $60,000 for a five-year contract, a record-setting salary for that time. Mikan proved to be worth every penny, because his presence brought so much attention and respect to the NBL. Mikan scored 100 points in his first five games and easily won the Most Valuable Player (MVP) trophy in 1946.

At that time, professional basketball was far from the hugely popular sport it is today. The NBL had only been around for nine years. Most of its teams were located in small cities, such as Fort Wayne, Indiana, and a few thousand spectators was considered an excellent crowd. Most professional players worked at other jobs during the off season. Mikan attended law school at DePaul when he was not playing.

"Mikan's arrival came at the right time for professional basketball," wrote Robert Peterson. "He was the game's first true superstar, and when he appeared on the scene, the pro game was poised to begin its bid for recognition as a major part of the national sports scene."[11]

In 1947, the owner of the American Gears decided to start his own league, with Mikan as his star attraction. However, the plan did not work out, and the American Gears ended up being disbanded. Mikan and the other players were distributed to other NBL teams. Mikan joined a new team called the Minneapolis Lakers.

The change in teams did not slow Mikan down. He led the Lakers to the NBL championship. Red Auerbach, later the famed coach of the Boston Celtics, stated that "George Mikan would have been a stickout performer anytime, anywhere, and under any conditions."[12]

More changes were in the air for Mikan and the Lakers. In 1948, the Lakers, along with three other teams, quit the NBL and joined a three-year-old league called the Basketball Association of America (BAA). As he had done with the NBL, Mikan's presence soon made the BAA the most popular professional basketball league. Finally, in 1949, the NBL and the BAA merged. The result was the National Basketball Association (NBA), which still dominates professional basketball today.

The Greatest

As he had done throughout his career, Mikan dominated the NBA. From 1948 to 1951, he averaged 28 points a game, and he led the Lakers to six NBA titles in his first nine seasons. He was such a high scorer that he was usually guarded by two or even three defenders. "He's six feet, ten inches," one reporter wrote, "and he couldn't be greater if he were ten feet, six inches."[13] In 1951,

Mikan prepares to shoot a basket as Nat "Sweetwater" Clifton unsuccessfully attempts to thwart the shot in a game on April 8, 1953. Most players had a difficult time defending the basket against Mikan.

Mikan was named the greatest basketball player of the first half of the twentieth century.

It was his amazing dominance on the court that led to the "George Mikan vs. the Knicks" announcement on the Madison Square Garden marquee. Mikan recalled being teased about that sign:

> Before the game against the Knicks that night, something odd happened. I had a habit of when I dressed before a game to place my eyeglasses on a locker shelf for safety. I'm very nearsighted and can hardly see without my glasses. I turned around. All of my teammates were still in street clothes. I said, "What's going on?" Sister Martin, our great guard, said: "George, didn't you see the marquee? It says you're playing the Knicks—go on out and play 'em." . . . Well, I gave them a few choice words, and we all broke out laughing.[14]

Although he was one of basketball's legends, Mikan is ultimately remembered for how he changed the way the game was played.

Mikan did more than score a lot of points. His style of play also changed league rules. Other players had so much trouble defending the basket against Mikan that the league doubled the width of the lane in front of the basket from six feet to twelve feet in 1951. This meant that Mikan had to take more shots from farther away from the basket. "It just forced me to be a better playmaker," Mikan said, "and I had some great teammates to pass to."[15]

Life away from the Basket

In 1954, at the age of thirty, Mikan decided to retire from professional basketball. He was tired of the constant physical punishment he endured during games. During his career, Mikan had suffered two broken legs, three broken fingers, a broken wrist, a broken nose, four broken teeth, and countless cuts, bumps, and bruises. Sportswriter Marc Pachter recalled that "Once, after a rival accused him of rough play, Mikan ripped off his shirt to reveal a torso covered with black-and-blue marks, and growled, 'What do you think these are—birthmarks?'"[16]

Of course, Mikan could give as much physical punishment to other players as he received himself. Former Boston Celtics player Ed Macauley once lost a tooth while defending against Mikan, and commented, "His elbows should be in the Hall of Fame."[17]

By 1954, the style of play in the NBA had changed. That year, the twenty-four-second clock was introduced. Now a team had to shoot at the basket within twenty-four seconds of gaining possession of the ball. This rule made basketball more exciting because it prevented teams from holding on to the ball and refusing to take a shot—and, therefore, not giving the other team a chance to get the ball. Mikan was not sure he could keep up with such a fast-paced, running game. It was time to move on.

Mikan stands outside his law offices. He opened a law practice after retiring from basketball in 1954.

Mikan also missed his family. "I came home one day and picked up my second son, Terry, and he began crying. He was afraid of me, because he didn't know who I was. It broke my heart."[18]

After he retired, Mikan started a law practice in Minneapolis and also ran unsuccessfully for Congress. He continued his close ties with professional basketball. His son Larry played basketball in the NBA. Mikan also served as the first commis-

20

sioner of the rival American Basketball Association (ABA) from 1967 to 1969.

Mikan was a key figure in bringing basketball back to Minnesota. During the 1980s, Mikan served as chairperson of a special state committee to start an NBA franchise in Minnesota. In 1989, the Minnesota Timberwolves began playing in Minneapolis. Twelve years later, on April 8, 2001, a life-size statue of George Mikan shooting his famous hook shot was erected in front of Target Stadium in Minneapolis, where the Timberwolves play. And in 1996 he was selected as one of the NBA's fifty greatest players.

During the 1990s, Mikan also became active in a new roller hockey league. He was part-owner and chairperson of the board of a team called the Chicago Cheetahs, which played in the Roller Hockey International league. Roller Hockey International was started by Dennis Murphy, who also founded the ABA. Murphy and Mikan had remained friends over the years, and when Murphy asked Mikan to buy a team, the former basketball star was happy to do so. "I'm having way too much fun at this," Mikan told a *Sports Illustrated* reporter in 1994. "And it's great to be back in Chicago. I get to lunch with Ray Meyer, my old DePaul coach, at least once a week."[19]

By 2001, Mikan was in poor health. He lost his right leg to diabetes and was on dialysis for kidney disease. But he continued to appear in public at half-time tribute ceremonies, and in basketball history, he remains a mighty figure.

George Mikan changed the game of basketball forever. He made the sport a game for big men, instead of a sport dominated by small, quick players. His style of play was so overwhelming that it forced both college and professional officials to change the rules. That, in turn, changed the style of play.

Mikan also helped to make the NBA popular. "Fans came out to see Mikan, first and foremost, and without a player of such magnitude, it is hard to imagine that the new leagues would have had much better prospects for survival than any of their forerunners. Mikan was such a drawing card that he quickly became almost bigger than the league itself."[20] Not a bad legacy for a nearsighted, clumsy kid who was told he was too tall to play basketball!

CHAPTER 2

Wilt Chamberlain: The Greatest Game of All

During the 1960s, the NBA increased in popularity. Several players stood out, achieving stunning records and amazing audiences with their style of play. One of the most exciting players of this era was Wilt Chamberlain. In 1962, he played one of the most memorable games of his career and set a record no one is ever likely to break.

Who Needs Basketball?

Wilton Norton Chamberlain was born in Philadelphia, Pennsylvania, on August 21, 1936. He and his ten brothers and sisters lived with their parents in a mostly black, working-class neighborhood. Chamberlain's father worked as a welder and a janitor, and his mother was a maid.

The Chamberlain family was not rich, but the parents made sure their children had what was important. "My folks managed," Wilt later recalled. "They didn't deny us anything that mattered. We always had clothes on our backs and food on the table."[21]

Chamberlain also credits his parents with giving him a sensible outlook about money:

> It's not the amount of money you have, it's what you do with it that brings pleasure and contentment. I owe this way of thinking to my mom and dad, who were two very giving people. Even though they had all us kids, and often there wasn't a lot to go around, they always had enough to share with neighbors or unexpected visitors. That has stayed with me, the feeling of wanting to share.[22]

The children also learned early that they had to work to help the family. Like his brothers and sisters, Chamberlain did chores around the house and also worked around the neighborhood for pay. He shoveled snow, carried groceries, and washed windows. "Jobs taught me the value of a dollar and the value of my own work,"[23] Chamberlain once said.

Although Chamberlain's parents were of average height and none of his brothers or sisters was exceptionally tall, Chamberlain was soon towering over other children his age. His childhood nickname was "Dipper," because he always had to dip down to pass through doorways. "At the age of fourteen I had almost reached my present-day height," Chamberlain wrote in his autobiography. "That's right, at fourteen I was seven feet tall."[24] Chamberlain also picked up another nickname—one he did not like as much as Dipper. Many people called him "Wilt the Stilt."

Most of the time, Chamberlain did not mind being so tall. "In those early days, around my friends and family I felt I was normal in height. It was only when I used to take the El (which was a subway above ground) to other parts of the city and I had to bend way over when standing in the compartment that I began to feel uncomfortable. If there were no empty seats, it seemed that *everyone* was staring at me."[25] Chamberlain also resented having to pay full price to get into the movies when children always got in for half price. No one could believe that someone that tall could still be a child.

A young Wilt Chamberlain poses for his school photo at West Overbrook High.

Chamberlain's height actually gave him some athletic advantages. While he was growing up, his favorite sport was track and field, and his long legs made him a natural at running and the high jump. He also enjoyed many other sports, especially football.

One sport Chamberlain had no time for was basketball. "I always thought it was a sissy game," he said. "It wasn't like running or football. I just didn't have any desire to play."[26]

By the time he was in junior high school, Chamberlain was tired of hearing he should play basketball and finally decided to give it a try. To his surprise, he loved the sport. Chamberlain quickly became a star on both local and school teams. In 1951, he helped his YMCA team to win a national tournament, even though the players on the other teams were much older.

During high school, Chamberlain's school had a 58–3 record over three years. They also won two Philadelphia city championships. Chamberlain was such a dominant player that it was not unusual for him to score 50 points in a game. Once he scored 73 points, and twice he scored 90 points. *Sport* magazine wrote an article about him called, "The High School Kid Who Could Play Pro Ball Now."[27]

College Days

Chamberlain was such a sensation that more than two hundred college recruiters attended his games during his senior year at West Overbrook High School. Professional teams were interested,

Chamberlain takes the rebound out of the hands of Roger Holloway at the NCAA Basketball Tournament at Oklahoma City University in 1957.

too. In 1955, an NBA team called the Philadelphia Warriors offered Chamberlain a professional contract. However, Chamberlain had just graduated from high school, and the rules at that time did not allow players to join the NBA at such a young age. Instead, Chamberlain went to the University of Kansas in Lawrence, Kansas.

Many people were surprised at Chamberlain's decision to attend a school that was not nationally known in basketball. However, Chamberlain was eager to play for Kansas coach Forrest Allen. "I went to the University of Kansas just because I respected their coach so much," Chamberlain later wrote in his autobiography. "He was Dr. Forrest C. Allen. He learned his basketball from a guy named Naismith [the inventor of basketball]—perhaps you've heard of him?"[28]

In at least one way, college was an eye-opening experience for Chamberlain. On his first day on campus, Chamberlain went to a restaurant in Lawrence to get some dinner. The owner refused to serve him because he was black. Chamberlain was furious at this racist treatment. He later recalled,

> It took me about a week to realize the whole area around Lawrence, except for one black section in Kansas City, was infested with segregation. I called on a few of the alums who had recruited me, and I told them in no uncertain terms what they could do with Kansas if things didn't get straightened out in a hurry. A couple of them told me, "Look, Wilt, you just go wherever you want. You sit down in those restaurants and don't leave until they serve you." That's exactly what I did. It took me about two months, but I went into every damn place within 40 miles of Lawrence, even places I didn't want to go into. I'd just sit there and glower and wait. Finally, they'd serve me. I never got turned down or bad-mouthed or anything, and when I got through, other blacks would follow me. I singlehandedly integrated that whole area.[29]

Chamberlain did not let his experiences with racism turn him against white people. He wrote,

> I think I have basketball to thank for not turning me into a bitter, vengeful black. I've had so many white coaches and teammates who became as close to me as brothers that it would be impossible for me to look on all whites as evil. . . . I pick my friends by their character, not their

color, and I haven't found that any one race has a monopoly on good *or* evil. I want good friends, warm friends, caring, loving, human friends—not black or white or purple friends. I felt that way before my experiences in Kansas, and I feel that way now.[30]

Chamberlain had an outstanding three years at the University of Kansas. School rules prevented Chamberlain from playing on the varsity team during his first year at the school, so instead he dominated the freshman team.

Chamberlain started his sophomore year by scoring 52 points and snatching 31 rebounds in his first game with the varsity team. He led Kansas to a 21-2 season and into the NCAA finals. Although Kansas lost the championship to North Carolina by one point, Chamberlain was named the tournament's MVP.

Chamberlain also had a good season during his junior year. However, he was getting bored with college ball. Also, Coach Allen had retired. Chamberlain was ready for something new. Since he could not play in the NBA yet, he decided to join the Harlem Globetrotters.

Globetrotting Wilt

The Harlem Globetrotters were a showcase team of black athletes who performed basketball exhibitions around the world. The team was known for its fancy ball handling and outrageous comedy routines. Joining the team gave Chamberlain the opportunity to get paid for playing ball and to travel around the world.

Chamberlain also saw the Globetrotters as a good way to prepare for the NBA. In an article for *Look* magazine, published shortly after he left Kansas, Chamberlain explained, "The game I was forced to play at K.U. wasn't basketball. It was hurting my chances of ever developing into a successful professional player."[31]

Years later, Chamberlain explained his reasons for leaving Kansas in more detail. "I was just 21 years old when I left Kansas," he recounted in his autobiography.

> If I'd gone straight into the NBA then, feeling as I did, I might never have made it. I might have cracked up under the rigors of an 82-game schedule and all the physical pummeling I'd have to take until I learned how to use my body and my elbows like the rest of the big men I'd be facing.[32]

During the 1958 season, Chamberlain toured Europe and the United States with the Globetrotters. Chamberlain had a good

Grasping two basketballs, Chamberlain poses as a member of the Harlem Globetrotters basketball team.

time and learned more about professional basketball. He also made enough money to buy his father a new car, as well as a house in a nice neighborhood for his parents. Chamberlain enjoyed his time with the Globetrotters so much that he continued to play with them during the summer for the next twelve years.

Turning Pro

In 1959, Chamberlain was finally eligible to play in the NBA. He joined the Philadelphia Warriors, who had drafted him four years earlier. Fans, athletes, and officials were excited to finally have this basketball sensation in the NBA. "He's great, that's all," said Boston Celtics coach Red Auerbach. "He'll take over this league."[33]

Auerbach's prediction came true. During the 1959–1960 season, Chamberlain averaged more than 37 points a game and had

Playing for the Philadelphia Warriors, Chamberlain tosses the ball in a game against the New York Knicks.

a league-leading 27 rebounds per game. At the end of the season, Chamberlain was named Rookie of the Year, Most Valuable Player, and All-NBA. He was the first player to ever win all those awards in one season.

The only weak part of Chamberlain's game was his foul shooting. He made only 58 percent of his foul shots. Chamberlain found this weakness frustrating. "I know the problem is all in my head," he said. "I shoot free throws well in practice."[34]

Although Chamberlain had an exceptional rookie season, he was not happy with the team. He felt his teammates did not work as hard as he did, complaining, "I'd play my heart out . . . and someone else on my team would blow the game." He also felt slighted by his coaches and the referees. "I don't like the way I'm coached. I'm not allowed to shoot when I have an open shot. The referees don't call fouls when other players push and shove me. My body aches all over." Chamberlain was sure that his size was partly to blame for the lack of respect. "The world is made up of Davids. I am a Goliath. And nobody roots for Goliath,"[35] he once said.

Things improved dramatically during Chamberlain's second season. In 1961 the Warriors got a new coach, Frank McGwire, who allowed Chamberlain more freedom on the court. McGwire also spoke up when he felt referees were not protecting Chamberlain from rough play. Chamberlain called McGwire "the finest man and the best coach I've ever played for."[36]

Inspired by a supportive coach and a better sense of teamwork among other players on the Warriors, Chamberlain had an incredible season during 1961–1962. He averaged a record 50.4 points a game and he was about to make basketball history.

The 100-Point Game

Chamberlain seemed to be unstoppable during the 1961–1962 season. Early in the season, he scored 73 points a game. Then, on December 8, 1961, he set an NBA record with 78 points during a triple-overtime game. After that game, McGwire told reporters, "Someday soon Chamberlain is going to score a hundred. He'll do it even if five men are guarding him."[37]

McGwire's prediction came true on March 2, 1962. That night, the Warriors were playing the New York Knicks in Hershey, Pennsylvania. Chamberlain's scoring rampage began almost at the opening buzzer. He scored 23 points in the first quarter and 18 more in the second. Chamberlain even made most of his foul shots, which were usually not his strong point.

By the time the second half started, everyone—the Warriors, the Knicks, and the spectators—was certain Chamberlain was going to break the scoring record. At the end of the third quarter, the Warriors led 125-106, and Chamberlain had 69 points.

With just eight minutes left in the game, Chamberlain broke his 78-point record. Although the crowd was excited, the Knicks were not happy. "After I broke the record of 78 points . . . the Knicks decided they didn't want someone to score 100 points against them," Chamberlain later explained.

The Knicks started to do anything they could to prevent me from getting 100 points. They'd foul my teammates intentionally so the ball wouldn't come to me. But they couldn't get the ball from [Warrior] Guy Rodgers, he was so fast. They couldn't even foul him. And when the ball got to me, they'd foul me immediately. They wouldn't even try to stop me. Just foul me and hope I missed the foul shots, but I didn't miss many. Down at the other end, the Knicks wouldn't shoot. They held the ball as long as they could to keep me from getting it. When I realized they didn't want me to score 100, that served as my motivation.[38]

Chamberlain scores his 100th point against the New York Knicks in Hershey, Pennsylvania, on March 2, 1962.

The big moment came with only forty-six seconds left to play. Chamberlain caught a pass from his teammate Joe Ruklick and stuffed it into the basket with both hands.

The crowd went wild. Although there was still time to play, so many fans ran onto the court that the game had to be stopped. Chamberlain retreated to the locker room, where he stayed so that the game could be completed. The final score was Warriors 169, Knicks 147.

Chamberlain was stunned by his achievement. "Honestly, I never thought I could do it," he told his teammates in the locker room. "Never in my life. It's really something. Like nothing that ever happened to me before. I sure feel different. Triple figures. Wow!"[39]

But Chamberlain also complained that the game was not his best. "It wasn't my most artistic game. I could have shot better, even though I impressed myself with my foul shooting. And the game itself, not just my part in it, was not particularly artistic. There were so many bad shots in the last quarter when the game got to be a real farce."[40] Despite his self-criticism, the 100-point game would go down in history, and it is a record that is likely to stand forever. The second-highest single-game score is Chamberlain's own 78 points in December 1961, and the modern game does not favor a single dominant shooter who takes enough shots at the basket to approach the record.

A Team Player

Although Chamberlain was an outstanding player who achieved many great feats on the basketball court, what he really wanted was to play for a championship team. Although the Warriors usually made it to the play-offs or the finals, they had never won the NBA championship. This losing streak continued even after the team moved to San Francisco for the 1962–1963 season. "I don't care about my points," Chamberlain often said. "All I care about is winning the NBA championship."[41]

In 1966, Chamberlain finally got a chance at the big time. He had been traded to a new team, the Philadelphia 76ers, in 1964. In 1966, the 76ers hired a new coach named Alex Hannum, along with several high-quality players. For the first time, Chamberlain was able to contribute as part of a team, not as an individual superstar. He enjoyed this new role and became one of the NBA's leading rebounders.

Chamberlain did not care that he was not scoring as many points as he had only a few years earlier. "My scoring went down only because I wanted it to, because it was what was best for my team," he explained. "I could always score 50 to 60 points if it was needed, but I knew my team was more effective if I sacrificed my scoring and passed and played defense."[42] Chamberlain's new sense of teamwork paid off when the 76ers defeated Chamberlain's old team, the San Francisco Warriors, in the NBA championships. Chamberlain was named MVP.

The following season, Chamberlain had 702 assists, the best in the NBA. "I got more happiness out of that record than almost any other record," he stated. "I showed people I could pass the ball to my teammates. The record proved I was more than a giant who could just dunk the ball. It proved I was willing to share the glory of winning."[43]

The End of a Career

Chamberlain was traded to the Los Angeles Lakers in 1969. Although the team played well, Chamberlain suffered a knee injury that almost ended his career. To continue playing basketball, he had to undergo an intense rehabilitation program. Chamberlain decided to do whatever was necessary to play basketball again.

As part of the Los Angeles Lakers, Chamberlain slaps away a hook shot made by Kareem Abdul-Jabbar during a 1972 NBA playoff game.

"Whatever they told me to do, I doubled it. If they said I should run five miles, I ran ten. If they said I should lift ten pounds with my leg, I lifted 20."[44] Chamberlain's hard work paid off, and he returned in time to take part in the play-offs. However, the Lakers lost to the New York Knicks in seven games.

In 1972, Chamberlain won his second NBA championship, defeating the Knicks. During the fifth game of the series, Chamberlain scored 24 points and had 29 rebounds. Few people knew it, but he was playing with a broken wrist, which had been injured in the previous game.

In 1973, Chamberlain surprised many people by retiring from basketball. "I could have signed another contract and made a lot more money," he explained. "In some ways I was getting better as a player. But I no longer found it fun to play. And too many hang on too long."[45]

Although Chamberlain is best remembered for his amazing 100-point game, he also set eleven other records, including most points in a season, highest scoring average, most field goals in a game, and the most career rebounds. He was especially proud of the record he set for playing in the most career games without fouling out—an amazing 1,045. "I'm proud of that record," he said. "I get paid to help my team. I can't help them if I'm on the bench or in the shower."[46]

Chamberlain also made basketball a faster, more exciting game and achieved enormous popularity all over the world. In 1978, he was elected to the Basketball Hall of Fame.

Chamberlain did not mind the idea of other athletes coming along and breaking his records. "I hope all my records are eventually broken," he wrote in his autobiography. "That's what records are for. If the players get better, that means the game gets better—and the fans have more fun."[47]

New Sports Passions

After he retired, Chamberlain remained active in sports. During his rehabilitation from the knee injury in 1972, he discovered beach volleyball. "I had the time of my life on the beach in bare feet and a pair of $2.98 shorts," he said. "I played volleyball all day, day after day. I found out just how little I really needed to be happy."[48]

Chamberlain also sponsored many women's sports teams. Growing up, his sisters had always been athletic, and Chamberlain felt that women's sports deserved more respect. "A couple of my sisters could have been great athletes . . . but in those days women didn't have many opportunities, especially women of

Chamberlain sits on the sidelines of a 1974 game as he coaches the San Diego Conquistadors. He remained active in sports after retiring from basketball.

color," Chamberlain wrote in his autobiography. "This is why I have always had a special place in my heart for women in sports, and why I've sponsored girls' volleyball teams. I have also coached some national volleyball champions and sponsored women's track and field teams."[49] Chamberlain also worked with Special Olympics and other children's charities.

During the early 1990s, Chamberlain tried his hand at acting. His first and most notable part was in *Conan the Destroyer*, which featured a fight scene between Chamberlain and action-film star

Arnold Schwarzenegger. Chamberlain found the experience entertaining and enjoyed the behind-the-scenes look at how movies were made.

Legacy of a Champion

Sports fans were shocked when news came that Chamberlain had died on October 12, 1999. He was sixty-three years old and had been suffering from congestive heart failure for several months.

Tributes poured in from around the world. Kareem Abdul-Jabbar, another great player who had broken Chamberlain's career scoring record in 1984, said, "Wilt was one of the greatest ever, and we will never see another one like him."[50] NBA commissioner David Stern put it best when he announced, "We've lost a giant of a man in every sense of the word. The shadow of accomplishment he cast over our game is unlikely ever to be matched."[51]

CHAPTER 3

Kareem Abdul-Jabbar: Scoring Champion

During the 1970s and 1980s, Kareem Abdul-Jabbar was a towering presence, both on and off the basketball court. His dramatic sky hook shot and extraordinary career point total made him an influential figure in the game. But Abdul-Jabbar also was a fighter off the court—fighting to win respect for black people throughout the country.

The Boy from New York City

Kareem Abdul-Jabbar was born Ferdinand Lewis Alcindor in New York City on April 16, 1947. He was an only child. Alcindor's father was a transit police officer and jazz musician, while his mother worked part-time as a cashier in a department store. The family lived in a middle-class housing project in the upper Manhattan neighborhood of Inwood.

Alcindor grew up in a multiracial neighborhood:

> It was a great environment to grow up in. We had the whole world in that project. We had immigrants from China, Russia, England, Scandinavia, Cuba. There were gypsies, Jews, West Indians, and American blacks. It was a cosmopolitan, multiethnic enclave. I got to play with kids of every description. It gave me an enduring tolerance and appreciation of differences, and an early awareness of how big the world was and how wide the range of human experience.[52]

However, growing up among a variety of different races and cultures did not shield Alcindor from racism. Like other African American families, the Alcindors became caught up in the struggle for civil rights that was going on in the United States during the 1950s. Like other black children, Alcindor had to endure the taunts of white children at school and in the neighborhood. "I never felt like I was black until I was made to,"[53] he later recalled.

As he grew older and taller, Alcindor was also teased about his size. By sixth grade, he was already over six feet tall. Alcindor found an ally in his mother, who was six feet tall:

> She was never comfortable with her size while she was growing up and was determined that not be the case with me. When I first started to dramatically outgrow my friends and questioned her about it, she told me to appreciate myself the way I was and to take pride in my height. She was emphatic about my standing up straight and walking tall.[54]

Making his debut in the NBA, Lew Alcindor is poised to try the sky hook shot he would become known for.

Alcindor's height also attracted attention from basketball coaches around the neighborhood and at St. Jude's Grammar School, the Catholic school Alcindor attended in the Bronx. Although Alcindor enjoyed basketball, he also enjoyed many other sports, including football, swimming, baseball, and ice skating.

An Awkward Star

Alcindor began playing basketball for Coach Farrell Hopkins at St. Jude's when he was in the fifth grade. He was awkward at that age and spent most of his time sitting on the bench. However, Hopkins took a special interest in Alcindor.

> I was at an age when my awkwardness could have become a trademark, and he gave me a confidence well beyond my

abilities just by letting me know that, no matter if I could dribble a ball or read one word, he was going to care about me. He was in a position to have a positive influence on a lot of kids, and he did.[55]

Hopkins spent extra time helping Alcindor to develop his abilities. Because he was so tall, Alcindor was able to "dunk" the ball, or jump higher than the basket and slam the ball through the hoop from above. In his autobiography, Alcindor recalled the first time he dunked a ball in a game:

I spent the whole summer practicing how to dunk, and when my eighth grade season started I finally had my chance in a game. One of my teammates, Patrick Dorish, had the ball on a fast break; there was one man back, and I was at the top of the key. Patrick drove, the man stayed with him, and as Patrick went by he just flipped me a pass and kept on going. The ball came up in my hands, I took one dribble and jammed it. The whole place went crazy.[56]

Alcindor also worked on another shot that would later become his specialty. He called it the sky hook. Alcindor described the first time he tried the sky hook, which involved soaring high in the air and sending the ball toward the basket in a long, curving arc. "I looked over my shoulder, saw the basket, turned into the lane, and with one hand put up my first hook shot. It missed, hit the back rim, and bounced out. But it felt right, and the next time I got the ball I tried it again. Neither of them went in, but I had found my shot."[57]

By the time he started high school at Power Memorial Academy in 1961, Alcindor was almost seven feet tall. He had also lost his awkwardness and grown into a powerful, graceful basketball player. However, Alcindor worried about fitting in at Power Memorial, which had a strong basketball program. "When I showed up at Power's first practices I was scared," he later wrote.

The game was too rough, and I didn't know how to be bad. I was not an aggressive boy, let alone an aggressive rebounder, and I think it must have showed on my face. I had size but no stature, and I was easily intimidated by guys who moved with authority. . . . People dunked over me and I couldn't do anything about it. I didn't move well to go get the ball, reaching with my arms instead of attacking with my whole body, and I had no idea how to make my presence felt.[58]

Alcindor blocks a competitor's shot during a game for Power Memorial High in 1964.

In spite of his doubts, Alcindor was chosen for the varsity team and soon became one of Power Memorial's star players. At age fourteen and six feet, ten inches tall, he was the team's starting center.

By his sophomore year, Alcindor was considered the most dominant high-school player in the country. During his four years at Power Memorial, he scored more than 2,000 points and led the team on a 71-game winning break. Power Memorial only lost one game in Alcindor's last three seasons.

Alcindor had a natural talent for the game, but he also knew he had to work hard to make the most of his abilities. Jack Donohue, the basketball coach at Power Memorial, remembered how Alcindor would put in extra practice time and never shied away from demanding workouts. "He never minded hard work," Donohue said. "He could run all day and he never complained about long practices."[59]

Black Power

The 1960s was a time of intense struggle and progress in the civil rights movement. While some groups stressed peaceful methods to win equality with whites, other groups had a more violent edge and called for "black power." During the summer of 1964, when Alcindor was seventeen years old, he was drawn to the black pride movement. "I was looking to grow into my culture,"[60] he later wrote.

Alcindor spent the summer working in the African American neighborhood of Harlem, in New York City. He joined the Harlem Youth Action Project, which was a city-run program for African American youths. Alcindor spent his days on the streets of Harlem, reporting on stories for the project's weekly newspaper. One of his most exciting moments was covering a press conference by Martin Luther King Jr.

Alcindor also took classes at the Schomburg Center for Research in Black Culture to get a better grasp of his heritage. The knowledge and experiences he gained helped Alcindor to mature. "I was anything but a Power Memorial junior; I was starting to feel like what I thought of as a man."[61]

The summer of 1964 was a violent time in Harlem. On July 18, riots broke out after a white police officer shot and killed an unarmed black teenager. Alcindor was caught in the thick of the violence and found himself filled with terror and anger. "It was chaos, wild and insane, and I just stood there trembling," he later recalled. "Absorbing what I'd seen . . . I knew it was rage, black rage." From then, "I was consumed and obsessed by my interest in black power, black pride, black courage."[62]

Off to California

Alcindor graduated from high school in 1965. Colleges from all over the nation wanted Alcindor, and recruiters bombarded him with attention. Alcindor's coach, Jack Donohue, tried to narrow down the choices to a few top schools. Even so, Alcindor and his parents were sometimes overwhelmed by the fancy promises they received.

> After a very short while, meeting with even the limited number of recruiters Coach Donohue permitted access to me, I became quite adept at intuiting out the phonies, the guys who had dollar signs or championship rings spinning in their eyes. Everyone I met with talked about how their concerns were for me and my education and my progress,

Alcindor towers over UCLA coach John Wooden as he receives some words of advice during a 1969 workout in Louisville, Kentucky.

but I knew quickly who was jive; it was something in the tone of voice—overstated authority or an air of desperation—and in the muscles at the side of the mouth that would pinch when I asked them about black players.[63]

In the end, Alcindor chose the University of California at Los Angeles (UCLA). UCLA's coach was John Wooden, one of the most respected and successful college basketball coaches of all time. He was also a strong advocate of black athletes. Alcindor explained, "I chose UCLA because it has the atmosphere I wanted, and because the people out there were very nice to me."[64]

NCAA rules did not allow Alcindor to play on UCLA's varsity team until he was a sophomore. But once he could play, it did not take long before Alcindor became the star of UCLA's basketball program. In his first game, he set a school record by scoring 56 points, a feat that was talked about all over the country. During his three years on UCLA's varsity team, the school won the NCAA championships three times and had an incredible 88-2 record. UCLA was the first college to win three NCAA championships in a row, and Alcindor became the first three-time MVP in NCAA history.

Alcindor's favorite shot was the dunk shot. Because he was just over seven feet tall, it was easy for him to slam the ball through the hoop. However, the NCAA felt that the shot made Alcindor *too* dominant and outlawed it from college play. Alcindor simply

Alcindor takes advantage of his height to keep control of the ball during a 1966 game against Duke University.

found new ways to score. He averaged 26 points a game through his college career.

The star player also developed a special relationship with his coach, John Wooden. In some ways, their connection to each other was surprising. "Our backgrounds were so different," Alcindor later recalled.

> I a child of the city and proudly black, he a country child from middle America, and a deacon in his church—and we were 37 years apart in age. Yet there was an immediate simpatico between our temperaments and a kind of pragmatic idealism that we shared. . . . I don't know why fate placed me in his hands, but I'm grateful that it did. My relationship with him has been one of the most significant of my life. He believed in what he was doing and in people. He had faith in us as players and as people. He was about winning in basketball and winning as human beings.[65]

A Higher Calling

Along with being a star basketball player, Alcindor was also a good student at UCLA. He majored in history and especially enjoyed studying black history and continuing to learn about his culture.

Alcindor also became fascinated by other religions. Although he had been raised as a Catholic, he found himself drawn to eastern religions, particularly Islam. He was especially inspired by the writings of black civil rights leader Malcolm X, who had been assassinated in

Deeply influenced by Malcolm X (pictured) and his Islamic teachings, Alcindor converted to Islam. In 1971, he took the Muslim name Kareem Abdul-Jabbar.

Harlem in 1965. Alcindor called Malcolm X "a profound influence"[66] on his life and his feelings about how whites and blacks should get along.

> Malcolm clearly showed what was right and what was wrong about what was happening here in America. And he opened the door for real cooperation between the races, not just the superficial, paternalistic thing. He was talking about real people doing real things, black pride, and Islam. I just grabbed on to it. And I have never looked back.[67]

Studying Malcolm X's teachings inspired Alcindor to read the Muslim holy book, the Koran. His teacher was a Muslim leader named Hamaas Abdul-Khaalis. In 1968, Alcindor converted to Islam and was given the Muslim name Kareem Abdul-Jabbar. In 1971, Alcindor legally changed his name.

The Milwaukee Bucks

In 1969, Abdul-Jabbar graduated from UCLA. He was ready for the NBA, and the NBA was ready for him. Abdul-Jabbar was the first pick in the NBA draft that year. He was chosen by the Milwaukee Bucks. The Bucks had been in last place the year before, but they hoped the addition of Abdul-Jabbar would improve the team's record. Abdul-Jabbar would be the Bucks' starting center.

Abdul-Jabbar's presence made an immediate difference to the team. During his first season, the Bucks won fifty-six games, which was twenty-nine more games than they had won the season before. Abdul-Jabbar averaged 29 points and 14 rebounds a game and was named the NBA's Rookie of the Year in 1970.

Abdul-Jabbar's proudest moment with the Bucks came in 1971, when the team won the NBA championship. Abdul-Jabbar was the league's top scorer and was widely considered to be the best player in the NBA. Although much of the credit for his excellent play came from natural talent, Abdul-Jabbar also had a reputation as a hard worker. It was not unusual for him to arrive at the gym four hours early, just to practice his shots.

Personal Troubles

Although Abdul-Jabbar excelled on the court during the early 1970s, his personal life was far from calm. He was still close to his Muslim adviser, Hamaas Abdul-Khaalis, and his mentor was pressuring him to marry according to Islamic tradition. He encouraged Abdul-Jabbar to marry a friend and fellow Muslim named Habiba Brown, even though Abdul-Jabbar was not certain that he

Abdul-Jabbar goes to the basket against Wilt Chamberlain in a 1970 Bucks-Lakers game. That year he was named NBA's Rookie of the Year.

loved her enough to make a lifelong commitment. However, he followed Abdul-Khaalis's advice. "I had my free choice; I could have done whatever I wanted," Abdul-Jabbar later wrote.

> But I didn't do what I wanted, didn't even really go off by myself and ponder this major question. As wealthy and powerful and celebrated as I was, I was still not capable of taking my life in my hands. Where was my strength, my confidence, my self-esteem? I permitted—encouraged— Hamaas to weigh a decision I was supposed to weigh. . . . I never questioned Hamaas. Finally, I did as I was advised.[68]

Abdul-Khaalis also insisted that the wedding take place with only Muslims present. Abdul-Jabbar's parents were not allowed to attend. Abdul-Jabbar recalled that after the ceremony, he heard that his parents were waiting outside.

> There were sharp words in the hallway. My mother and father, who had left New York at midnight and driven five hours to get there, had not been told in advance that they would not be permitted at the ceremony and were being barred at the door. I hadn't known that they would be denied entrance. This wasn't the kind of wedding I had fantasized about.[69]

The incident caused a break between Abdul-Jabbar and his parents that lasted for eleven years.

Then, on January 18, 1973, Abdul-Jabbar was touched by tragedy when several of Abdul-Khaalis's children and grandchildren were massacred by a rival group of black Muslims. The attack took place in a house Abdul-Jabbar had bought for Abdul-Khaalis in Washington, D.C. Abdul-Khaalis escaped the attack because he was not home. Officials thought that Abdul-Jabbar might also be a target for assassination, so he was given around-the-clock police protection.

After the attacks, Abdul-Jabbar began to reevaluate his relationship with Abdul-Khaalis. His studies of Islam taught him that many of the things his spiritual leader had said were not actually part of Islamic law. Abdul-Jabbar realized that he had to take control of his own life, instead of relying on someone else to tell him what to do. "I gave a large portion of my life over to Hamaas, and he taught me most of the ideas I now hold most strongly," Abdul-Jabbar reflected in his autobiography.

> But . . . I can't agree with or accept everything that Hamaas did; if I could, life would be real easy, but I can't. I've had to realize that and step back, allow Hamaas to live according to what he believes is right, and insist that he and everybody else allow me to make my own decisions and live by my own rights.[70]

Abdul-Jabbar also separated from his wife, saying, "It was not a difficult decision; I was erasing a mistake."[71]

Trouble on the Court

The turmoil in Abdul-Jabbar's personal life began to affect his play on the basketball court. In 1975, he decided he wanted to return to Los Angeles and asked the Milwaukee Bucks to trade him to the Los Angeles Lakers. The team agreed, and Abdul-Jabbar headed west.

Abdul-Jabbar was a sensation with the Lakers, just as he had been with the Bucks. Once again, he led the league in scoring every year and won two more MVP awards.

Despite his acclaim, Abdul-Jabbar felt he was treated unfairly by the press and other players. He had long felt that officials allowed other players to jab him in the ribs or hit him in the head without being called for fouls, simply because Abdul-Jabbar was so tall.

Sporting protective goggles, Abdul-Jabbar shoots a sky hook in a game against the Utah Jazz in Las Vegas on April 6, 1984.

Getting battered intentionally by two-hundred-twenty-pound athletes eighty-two games per season . . . is no day at the beach. I've had both eyes gouged—I wear protective goggles every game because that's where I am most vulnerable—I've been punched, pulled, pinched, pummeled. The concept is I'm so big that that's the only way you can beat me, but it's dangerous and it hurts. Out on the court I am my only defender.[72]

In 1977, Abdul-Jabbar had finally had enough. During a game in Milwaukee, Abdul-Jabbar was elbowed in the stomach by a young player named Kent Benson. Abdul-Jabbar reacted by punching Benson in the eye. He broke his hand in the process and was unable to play for several weeks.

Fans and journalists rushed to criticize Abdul-Jabbar's actions. Abdul-Jabbar was not proud of himself either:

> I was angry and confused. I had been attacked, had responded in my own defense, and once again had become the villain. My temper had gone out of control and taken my newfound relaxation with it. I knew I could count on even more public hostility now. I certainly got it. Boos from the crowds, columnists calling me a coward. . . . I wasn't very pleased with myself for having lost control . . . and I resolved to hold my temper better in the future. I haven't had a serious fight since.[73]

Abdul-Jabbar was also helped by his girlfriend, Cheryl Pistano, who worked with him to manage his anger. "I realized, with my hand broken and reputation damaged, that my temper could ruin my career and that I'd have to control it, but Cheryl went deeper and told me that I was missing out on not only my career but my whole peace of mind."[74] Pistano also helped to mend the rift between Abdul-Jabbar and his parents.

Holding his sixth MVP award, Abdul-Jabbar smiles at an NBA luncheon in Los Angeles.

Reaching New Heights

Abdul-Jabbar had a much more positive outlook on his life and his career during the 1980s, and those years became his most successful ever. The Lakers won five championships between 1980 and 1988, and Abdul-Jabbar received his sixth MVP award, breaking an NBA record. In 1985, Abdul-Jabbar was named *Sports Illustrated*'s Sportsman of the Year.

Although he was now in his late thirties, Abdul-Jabbar continued to be the NBA's top scorer. Lakers coach Pat Riley called his sky hook "the most awesome weapon in the history of any sport"[75] and assistant coach Bill Bertka said it was "the most indefensible shot in basketball."[76]

On April 5, 1984, Abdul-Jabbar made NBA history. Until that day, Wilt Chamberlain held the all-time NBA career-scoring record with 31,419 points. That night, facing the Utah Jazz, Abdul-Jabbar was only twenty points behind Chamberlain's record.

Abdul-Jabbar tied the record during the fourth quarter. Although he was triple-teamed by Utah's defense, Abdul-Jabbar managed to grab a pass from teammate Magic Johnson and launch it toward the basket from twelve feet away, using his famous sky hook shot. The ball went through the hoop and Abdul-Jabbar became the new scoring champion. By the time he retired in 1989, Abdul-Jabbar's point total was an astounding 38,387, which is still a record today.

Losing Everything

The 1980s were a time of great professional success for Abdul-Jabbar. However, he suffered a devastating blow in January 1983, when an electrical fire destroyed his home in Los Angeles while Abdul-Jabbar was on the road with the Lakers. Although his girlfriend, Cheryl Pistano, and their young son, Amir, escaped without injury, everything in the house was destroyed. "It looked like somebody had dropped a bomb on it," Abdul-Jabbar later wrote.

> The house and everything in it, everything I owned, a lifetime of possessions, my book and music libraries, priceless Korans, the jazz collections I'd started in high school, my Asian and Middle Eastern rugs, old photographs, my wardrobe, every sock, every dish, all had been incinerated. In an instant, my material world had been reduced to a carry-on bag, the few things that I had brought with me on the road. It was a neat statement on life.[77]

Losing his material possessions in the fire changed Abdul-Jabbar's priorities:

> Cheryl and Amir had gotten out alive, and when placed next to life itself my possessions began to seem rather small. With so little left, I found I hadn't really needed much of what I'd collected and owned. Material possessions, which had been a mark of both success and contentment to me, lost some power once they were gone.[78]

Abdul-Jabbar appears in the film Airplane. *In addition to working as an actor, Abdul-Jabbar is also actively involved in movie production.*

Retiring from the Game

In 1989, at the age of forty-two, Abdul-Jabbar was finally ready to retire. He had been playing professional basketball for twenty years and held the record for the most games played with 1,560.

When Abdul-Jabbar announced that the 1988–1989 season would be his last, the season became a farewell tour. Abdul-Jabbar was honored by teams all over the United States and received standing ovations, testimonials, and gifts from players and fans.

When he left the sport, Abdul-Jabbar reflected: "Now it's time to let one life end and see what happens in my new life as a regular citizen. The sport goes on. People will find new heroes. And I'm flattered they'll be compared to me. That's something I can enjoy for the rest of my life, as I will the memory of my last time around the league and the late-autumn sunshine I received from the fans."[79]

Abdul-Jabbar has had a busy retirement. He has remained active in sports, including wind surfing, weight training, yoga, and swimming. He has also written two autobiographies and remains politically active as president of Kareem Productions, a company that produces movies about the black experience. Abdul-Jabbar also turned to acting, with roles in many TV shows and movies as well as television commercial appearances.

Abdul-Jabbar has not forgotten basketball. In 1995, he joined a group of former NBA players to defeat the Harlem Globetrotters. He would also like to coach someday, saying, "I see a great need for people to teach the game. I don't think young people are getting the fundamentals."[80]

Most of all, Abdul-Jabbar is aware of his place in basketball history. When he was growing up in New York City, he had the opportunity to see the stars of the 1950s play. Now, Abdul-Jabbar can sit back and watch today's NBA superstars and know that they are following in his large footsteps.

CHAPTER 4

Magic Johnson: Making Things Happen

His brilliant smile and outstanding play made Magic Johnson one of the most exciting players to watch on the basketball court. Johnson was a man who made things happen and had fun doing it. But in 1991, while he was at the height of his popularity, Johnson was forced to retire and change his life completely because of a deadly and much-feared disease. He went on to show that he could accomplish great things off the court as well.

A Young Player

Earvin Johnson grew up in Lansing, Michigan, where he was born on August 14, 1959. He later described his family as

> the kind of black family that people today worry is disappearing. Even though there were nine of us, we had what we needed—two great parents, food on the table, and time for the whole family to be together. To provide for us, my parents worked terribly hard. My father had two full-time jobs, and Mom worked just as hard to keep the household going. Seven kids kept her busy, but she also had jobs outside the home.[81]

Lansing is an hour and a half from Detroit, home of the NBA Pistons. Johnson loved the Pistons, and attending their games was one of the highlights of his childhood. In those days, tickets were cheaper and more available than they are today, so Johnson was able to enjoy many Pistons' games.

Later, Johnson would take the moves he had seen at NBA games and use them on the neighborhood basketball courts. He dreamed of being an NBA star like his heroes. Johnson never dreamed that someday he would be an NBA star whom other kids would look up to.

Johnson also learned some important basketball lessons from his father. Basketball created a special bond between father and son. Although his father did not have much free time because of his demanding work schedule, he always spent Sunday afternoons watching NBA games on television with his son. After the game, the two would often go to the local basketball courts and play one-on-one.

From an early age, Earvin "Magic" Johnson was intrigued by basketball.

> He taught me how to be aggressive on the court: how to drive to the basket and take the charge; how to put up a shot as I was being hit. . . . He taught me to win against the odds, and never to quit. It was years before I was finally able to beat him one-on-one. But when I did, I knew I had really earned it. Physically, I'm not the most gifted basketball player in the world. I've never been the fastest runner or the highest jumper. But thanks to my father, nobody will ever outsmart me on the court.[82]

It was not long before every free moment Johnson had was consumed by basketball. His family and neighbors could always find Johnson by following the sound of a bouncing basketball.

> No matter what else I was doing, I always had a basketball in my hand. . . . I remember waking up when it was still dark outside and wanting to play ball so badly that I'd just lie there, looking out the window, waiting for daybreak. If it was too early to go to the schoolyard, I'd dribble on the street. I'd run around the parked cars and pretend they were players on the other team. All up and down Middle Street people used to open their windows and yell at me for waking them up. But I couldn't help it. The game was just in me.[83]

On rainy days, Johnson played in the house by rolling up some socks and tossing them at a square he had drawn on the wall.

A Standout in the Schoolyard

By the time he started seventh grade, Johnson was six feet, three inches tall and towered over his classmates. His size, ability, and

A beaming Johnson stands with his father at New York's Plaza Hotel, where he was chosen by the Lakers in the first round of the NBA draft.

determination made him the star of any neighborhood basketball game. He played in every local league and neighborhood pickup game he could find. Johnson even played with older kids who were in high school.

Playing with older kids helped to shape Johnson's game. Because he was younger, the other players did not always welcome him on the court. However, Johnson soon learned that if he passed the ball to his teammates instead of trying to take every shot himself, they were more likely to let him on the court. Clearly, being a team player was the key to success. This was a lesson Johnson never forgot, and it was a principle that would shape his playing style throughout his career.

Johnson joined his junior high team in seventh grade. It was not unusual for him to score 30 points in a game. After one game when he broke the school's single-game scoring record with 48 points, the whole community was talking about Johnson's amazing abilities.

Johnson's parents were proud of their son, but they never let all the attention spoil him:

> My family always supported me, but they never let me get
> a swelled head. Maybe I was the hero of the game, but

when I got home I still had to take out the trash. . . . Even though people made a big fuss about me in junior high, I didn't believe I was as good as they said. . . . I always had doubts about myself, but that turned out to be a big advantage. It kept my expectations low, and it made me work like crazy to keep getting better.[84]

A Sudden Change of Plans

Johnson looked forward to attending Sexton High School, which had one of the best basketball teams in Michigan. However, before he started high school, the city began a court-ordered busing program to integrate Lansing's schools. Instead of going to all-black Sexton, which was only five blocks from Johnson's home, he would have to take a bus to Everett High School, an all-white school on the other side of town.

Johnson was furious at the idea of attending a white school. Even more upsetting was the fact that Everett had a terrible basketball team. Johnson did everything he could to avoid going to Everett. He claimed that his family had moved, and that he was living with friends in another part of the neighborhood. He even appealed to the school board, but nothing worked. Johnson would go to Everett, whether he liked it or not.

Later, Johnson realized that being forced to go to Everett was a good thing:

As I look back on it today, I see the whole picture very differently. It's true that I hated missing out on Sexton. And for the first few months, I was miserable at Everett. But being bused to Everett turned out to be one of the best things that ever happened to me. It got me out of my own little world and taught me how to understand white people, how to communicate and deal with them.[85]

One of the first people Johnson had to learn to deal with was his basketball coach, George Fox. Fox was an old-fashioned coach who stressed the fundamentals and did not believe in the flashy, creative plays that were popular among black athletes at the school. He often criticized Johnson for playing a so-called running game. Johnson's style included quick passes, behind-the-back dribbles, and electrifying jump shots. To Fox, this was not good basketball. It was just showing off.

Although the two clashed at first, in time they came to respect each other. Both of them appreciated dedication and hard work. "George Fox was a good coach and an excellent teacher," Johnson

Playing for Michigan State, Johnson drives past Western Kentucky's Darryl Turner on his way to the basket.

later wrote in his autobiography. "He worked us hard and stressed the fundamentals. . . . Although talent is important, the fundamentals will usually win out. And nothing in the world beats hard work."[86] In turn, Fox realized that Johnson's style helped the team to score and changed his opinion about his star player.

Johnson also credits Fox with helping him to find his best position on the court. Fox was the first person to realize Johnson played best as a guard, not a forward or a center. Soon Johnson had the reputation of being not only an excellent athlete but also an excellent playmaker.

Along with adjusting to a new coach, Johnson also had to cope with playing for a mostly white team and attending a mostly white school. At first, many of his white teammates "froze him out" during practices. They refused to pass the ball to Johnson or let him participate in important plays. Fortunately, Johnson was supported by his coach and a few of his white teammates, and things eventually became easier.

Johnson also faced racist attitudes from members of the school's staff. Perhaps his greatest challenge came from a school security guard nicknamed John the Narc. "John didn't like me," Johnson later wrote.

Maybe he resented all the attention I was getting. Or maybe it was good old-fashioned prejudice. Whatever the reason, he loved to tell me that I would never amount to anything. "You think you're really something because you can play ball," he'd say. "But you'll see. You won't even graduate from here. No black kid ever comes out of here and is successful. You're just like the rest of them." I hated him, but I never said a word. I figured that he was dying for me to talk back so he could get me in trouble. Instead of responding, I just let it wash over me. . . . John the Narc would be shocked to hear it, but I turned him from my enemy into my biggest motivator.[87]

Because of his exceptional ability on the court, Johnson received the nickname "Magic."

A Magical Night

Until his first year of high school, Johnson had simply been called by his first name, Earvin, or his initials, E.J. However, his amazing basketball talents made some people feel that he deserved a more memorable nickname.

Everett had never had a very good basketball team, but with Johnson leading the way, the team began winning game after game. During one game, Johnson had one of the best games of his life, scoring 36 points and snagging 18 rebounds and 16 assists. After the game, Fred Stabley Jr., a sportswriter for the *Lansing State Journal*, stopped to talk to Johnson in the locker room. He told the young ballplayer he should have a nickname, and suggested "Magic." Johnson didn't think much of the idea, but he agreed. Stabley began referring to Johnson as "Magic" in his articles. Within two months Magic Johnson was a name every basketball fan in Michigan recognized.

Johnson realized that his new nickname made people expect even more of him. "The name became a challenge, and I love challenges."[88] Johnson's determination motivated his teammates as well, and Everett—once the laughingstock of the city's sports teams—became a basketball powerhouse. The high point of Johnson's high school career was when his school won the state championship during his senior year.

A Surprising Choice

As Johnson's high school career came to a close, it was time for him to take his magic touch to college. Johnson had worked as hard in the classroom as he had on the basketball court, and his combination of excellent grades and amazing athletic ability meant that he could have attended any school in the country. Many people thought he would choose a powerhouse basketball school, such as UCLA, Indiana University, or the University of North Carolina. However, Johnson had another school in mind: Michigan State.

Michigan State did not have as mighty a basketball program as other schools. However, Johnson had played in many pickup games at the school and attended basketball camps there. Michigan State felt like a second home. Because Michigan State was near Lansing, Johnson's family, friends, and members of the community also wanted him to attend.

Johnson was also encouraged to attend Michigan State after talking to the school's coach, Jud Heathcote. Heathcote told Johnson that if he played for Michigan State, he would make a huge difference to the team. Johnson loved the idea of choosing to play for the weaker team, and making them better just as he had done at Everett.

It did not take long for Johnson's plans and dreams for the Michigan State team to come true. After his first season, the school had a 25-5 record, which was a big improvement over the previous year. Johnson, playing point guard (a position that involves running the offense and setting up scoring opportunities), averaged 17 points a game. He was named to the All Big Ten team at the end of the season.

Magic's teammates were impressed by his playmaking abilities. One of his teammates, Terry Donnelly, said, "You're running down the floor, and you're open and most people can't get the ball to you through two or three people, but all of a sudden the ball's in your hands and you've got a layup."[89]

At the end of the season, Johnson received a tempting offer when the NBA's Kansas City Kings invited him to join their team. If he did, Johnson would be the youngest player in the NBA. However, Johnson did not feel he was physically or mentally ready for the NBA, and he was enjoying his life at Michigan State too much to give it up. Instead of going pro, Johnson went back to college for his sophomore year.

A National Sensation

Johnson had been popular throughout Michigan for many years. However, his fame spread nationwide after *Sports Illustrated* magazine featured him on the cover of its November 27, 1978, issue. "The article was a profile of the top ten sophomore players in the country," Johnson recalled.

> I was described exactly how I like to see myself—as a winner. "Opponents have learned that they may be able to outrun, outjump, outmuscle, or outshoot Johnson," it said. "But it is almost impossible to beat him.". . . [The cover] changed my life. Within weeks, I went from being known throughout Michigan to being recognized all over the country.[90]

Despite the national attention, Johnson's sophomore season at Michigan State got off to a rocky start. Although the team was ranked number one in the country, they were losing most of their games. Johnson believed that the reason for the team's slump was Coach Heathcote. Heathcote favored a slow style of play that protected the ball. Johnson thought the team should play more aggressively and move the ball quickly down the court.

When Heathcote called a team meeting, Johnson and his teammates all told the coach that they felt his style was slowing the game down and hurting the team. Although Heathcote could be stubborn, he knew how to listen. After listening to his team, Healthcote changed his style and encouraged his team to be more aggressive. The results took Michigan State all the way to the NCAA finals.

Johnson leaps toward the basket during the 1979 NCAA Basketball Tournament. He was named MVP.

The championship game was played on March 26, 1979, and featured Michigan State against Indiana State. The nation was so excited by Johnson's flashy style and personality that, as sportswriter Herzog notes, the game "spawned a national love affair with basketball."[91] The game had the largest television audience ever to watch a tournament. Johnson scored 24 points and Michigan State won the game, 75-64, but the real winner was college basketball itself. Author Roy S. Johnson said, "That game was the turning point for what we now know as March Madness. It wasn't always March Madness. It was just the NCAA Tournament. But after that, it became every little boy's dream to play in that game."[92]

Magic and the Lakers

After his sophomore year of college, Johnson felt that he was ready for the NBA. He was drafted by the Los Angeles Lakers. Although many people were disappointed that Johnson was leaving school after only two years, Johnson believed that it was time to move on. The Lakers was a strong team, and NBA procedures meant that Johnson might be drafted by a weaker team if he waited one more year. Johnson also looked forward to playing with Kareem Abdul-Jabbar, the Lakers' star center. "The Lakers . . . had Kareem Abdul-Jabbar, the foremost player in all of basketball. If he and I could develop some chemistry on the court, and I could feed the ball to Kareem . . . the results could be very interesting,"[93] Johnson wrote in his autobiography.

Johnson was an instant sensation in the NBA. He played hard, but he had a good time. "It's a good thing I do not mind getting knocked down," Johnson later wrote. "I took a real beating that first year, but I played hard, and missed only five games due to injuries. I loved being a member of the Lakers, and I couldn't wait for the games."[94] His enthusiastic attitude and energy helped Johnson to adjust to the rigors of professional basketball. And fans could not get enough of Johnson's megawatt smile. No one had ever seen an athlete who enjoyed playing as much. "Magic laughs out there on the court simply from the joy of the game,"[95] sportswriter Dave Anderson once wrote.

Johnson won his first NBA championship ring during his rookie season with the Lakers. After the team defeated the Philadelphia 76ers in six games, and Johnson scored 42 points in the final game, his coach, Paul Westhead, said, "Magic thinks every season goes like that. You play some games, win the title, and get named MVP."[96] And Lionel Hollins of the 76ers simply said, "Magic. He is his name."[97]

However, Johnson received a lot of criticism during his second season with the Lakers. He missed forty-five games with a knee injury, then signed a $25 million contract with the Lakers. Sportswriters and fans wondered why he was being paid more than Kareem Abdul-Jabbar.

Johnson stands proudly with Sport *magazine's Most Valuable Player trophy after an excellent rookie year.*

Things only got worse when Johnson complained about his coach, Paul Westhead. After the two disagreed about how to run the team's offense, Johnson told reporters he wanted to be traded to another team. The next day, Westhead was fired. Jim Murray of the *Los Angeles Times* wrote, "Now we know why they call him Magic. He made the boss disappear."[98]

But the fans could not stay angry at Johnson for long. It helped that Westhead's replacement, Pat Riley, made the Lakers a more powerful team.

Johnson had a sensational eleven-year career with the Lakers. The team made it to the NBA finals nine times and won the championship five times. Johnson was named league MVP three times and playoff MVP three times. He averaged more than 19 points a game and created a new record of 136 triple doubles (10 or more points, rebounds, and assists in one game). "When he's in control," said Boston Celtics coach K.C. Jones, "there's no one like him."[99] "Magic is aware of everybody," said Lakers assistant coach Bill Bertka. "Magic sees everything, and he understands everything he sees."[100]

Then, on November 7, 1991, something happened that brought Johnson's career, confidence, and public image crashing down around him.

A Stunning Announcement

In October 1991, Johnson underwent a physical exam and blood test to qualify for a life insurance policy. The exam was routine and Johnson felt perfectly healthy, so he was not worried about the results. Then, on October 25, while Johnson was on the road with the Lakers, the team's physician called Johnson and insisted that he return to Los Angeles immediately. Johnson had failed the physical. The reason was shocking—he had tested positive for HIV, the virus that causes AIDS.

Johnson was stunned. Like many people at the time, he knew that HIV was a deadly virus spread by sexual contact and infected blood, but he assumed that HIV was primarily a disease of homosexuals or drug users, not spread by heterosexual contact. As a star athlete, Johnson had had opportunities for casual sexual relationships with many women, and he acted on them. "I know *how* I got HIV. That's clear," he wrote in his autobiography.

> But I do not know who gave it to me. I called a number of women before I made the announcement, so they could get tested. I also called women after the announcement. They

Before a crowded room, Johnson announces his retirement from the NBA after learning that he tested positive for HIV.

knew about it by then, of course, but I still felt some responsibility toward them. Of the women I have talked to, nobody has tested positive—at least not yet.[101]

Johnson was especially worried about one woman: Earletha "Cookie" Johnson. Cookie and Johnson had met at Michigan State and had dated off and on over the years. A few months earlier, they had married. Cookie was now six weeks pregnant with their first child. Johnson was relieved when she tested negative for HIV. The baby, a boy, was born healthy.

On November 7, Johnson called a press conference and told the world he was HIV-positive. "There was never any question that I would go public with it," he later wrote.

> I doubt I could have kept it quiet. Besides, I've never lied to people, and I didn't want to start now. I've always lived straight ahead, facing up to whatever happens. There was another reason I wanted to make this announcement. Despite all the warnings, a lot of other people were living the way I had—especially athletes and entertainers. . . . This had happened to me, and there wasn't too much I could do about that. But there was a great deal I could do for other people. By going public with this, I had a chance to save lives.[102]

To do this, Johnson said he was going to form a foundation to fund AIDS research, and that he would work to increase AIDS awareness among young people.

Johnson also announced that he was retiring from basketball. Although doctors felt they had caught the virus early and Johnson was still in good health, everyone agreed that playing would put too much stress on Johnson's body, especially his immune system. There was also the fear that Johnson might be injured on the court and bleed onto another player or official, possibly contaminating them with the virus. Although the odds of this happening were very small, the fear was very big.

The press conference stunned people around the world. It also stirred up controversy. In some ways, Johnson's bombshell humanized the face of AIDS. "Sometimes we think only gay people can get it, or it's not going to happen to me," Johnson said during his speech. "Here I am, saying it can happen to everybody. Even me, Magic Johnson."[103]

Leigh Montville wrote in *Sports Illustrated* that Johnson had "probably spent more time with us—and we have spent more time

George H.W. Bush meets with Johnson during Johnson's first day as a member of the president's National Commission on AIDS.

with him—than most of our blood relatives. Now he was sick? A disease that we had viewed mostly with passive dismay was suddenly immediate, real."[104] Another *Sports Illustrated* writer, Jack McCallum, stated, "Whether you were shaking your head at his indiscretions or weeping at his misfortune, you couldn't deny the cruel irony of the revelation: one of the best, and best-loved, athletes on earth had contracted this horrible virus."[105]

Some people were impressed by Johnson's honesty and thought that his presence would be a huge benefit to AIDS research. At the time, AIDS victims were feared and ostracized by much of society. Having a popular celebrity with the virus could change public perceptions. "If the people battling HIV had called central casting to summon the perfect spokesman, they could not have improved upon Magic Johnson," said AIDS activist Randy Shilts. "No human being in the history of the AIDS epidemic is better positioned to get the battle against AIDS moving."[106]

But to others, Johnson's public image was tarnished if not ruined by the fact of sexual promiscuity. To these people, Johnson was far from someone to be admired. "Johnson has not been a hero to women. He has been a hazard,"[107] wrote Sally Jenkins in *Sports Illustrated*.

No matter what people were saying about him, Johnson was determined to fight back against AIDS. As he had promised during his press conference, Johnson formed the Magic Johnson Foundation to fund AIDS research. He also worked to increase AIDS awareness among young people, creating an informational television show and writing a book. Johnson was also appointed to the president's National Commission on AIDS, but resigned less than a year later because he did not agree with the commission's approach to educating the public and preventing the spread of AIDS.

Back to Basketball

Johnson also made his own health a priority. Doctors prescribed a number of drugs to keep his immune system working, and he followed a healthy diet and exercise program. As he remained healthy and strong, Johnson began to miss playing basketball. He also thought he could show people that being HIV-positive did not have to prevent a person from living an active life.

In 1992, Johnson worked as a commentator for NBC's professional basketball telecasts, but he longed to return to the court. That winter, he played in the NBA All-Star Game and was named MVP. He also played without incident on the U.S. Olympic Team at the Summer Olympics in Barcelona, and helped the team to win a gold medal.

Encouraged by these successes, Johnson announced that he was returning to the Lakers during the 1992–1993 season. "I could still play, and the joy of playing is so much in my blood," he wrote. "I started asking myself: Why am I not playing? Finally, with the new season only a few weeks away, I called a press conference to announce that I was coming back. God put me here to play basketball and to do my thing on the court."[108]

But returning to the game was more complicated than Johnson had anticipated. Although doctors and other medical experts said that there was little chance Johnson could infect other players, many athletes admitted they were nervous about being on the court with him. Johnson realized that having the desire and ability to play was not enough. Two months after the start of the season, he announced his second retirement from the sport he loved. Dr. David E. Rogers, vice chairperson of the National Commission of AIDS and the NBA's first AIDS adviser, said that the "unreasonable fears . . . of his fellow players did something to him that the AIDS virus couldn't. It made him quit."[109]

"They took away so much from me," Johnson later said. "The basketball, the commercials, the love I had for the game. I figured

Starbucks business partner Magic Johnson co-hosts the company's thirtieth anniversary celebration in Seattle, outside the corporation's first store.

I would play five, six more years. I quit for one reason and one reason only: The controversy was hurting the game. Quitting was the right thing to do, but it hurt."[110]

Still Making a Difference

Even after his basketball career ended, Johnson remained in the public eye. Of course, he spent much of his time working on AIDS awareness and education. Johnson also dedicated his time and money to improving black communities around the United States. Magic Johnson Enterprises is a $500 million empire of shopping plazas, movie theaters, and restaurants, all located in black communities such as Harlem in New York City. These businesses have brought money, jobs, and self-esteem into communities around the country.

Johnson also wants young black people to have goals and to take responsibility for their own success, in spite of racism or other disadvantages. In "A Message for Black Teenagers" in his autobiography, Johnson wrote,

You can still walk proud because of who you are. If we keep using that same old excuse, that every time we fail it's because of racism, we'll never get ahead. We'll stay on the bottom. We've got to quit making excuses. Quit feeling sorry for ourselves. . . . The government will not save you. The black leadership will not save you. You're the only one who can make the difference. Whatever your dream is, go for it.[111]

Magic Johnson's life has been an incredible adventure, both on and off the court. No matter what challenges he faced, he proved he was a champion at the game of basketball and, more important, at the game of life.

CHAPTER 5

John Stockton: A True Team Player

Many NBA stars are known for their commanding presence, flashy style, and superstar attitude. But it is possible to be great in a quieter way. Although he is often overlooked, John Stockton is one of the sport's best athletes and the ideal model of a team player who makes essential contributions to every game.

Quiet Determination

John Houston Stockton was born on March 26, 1962, in Spokane, Washington. His father was the co-owner of a bar called Jack and Dan's Tavern, while his mother was a homemaker. The Stockton family included four children: John; older brother, Steve; older sister, Stacy; and younger sister, Leanne. The family was loving and relaxed, and their Roman Catholic faith was an important part of their lives. Stockton's neighborhood was so heavily Catholic that it was sometimes called Little Vatican. "I feel very lucky to have grown up where I did, and the way I did,"[112] Stockton once said.

Stockton was interested in basketball almost as soon as he could walk. During his childhood, he spent hours shooting at a basketball hoop in his driveway. Neighbors soon became used to hearing the sounds of Stockton dribbling and shooting until late at night. The young boy even played in heavy rain or snow.

Stockton's first opponent was his brother, Steve, who was four years older. Steve was not only older but also much bigger, and he did not hesitate to push John around. "Those were rough games and I'd get knocked around," Stockton recalled. "Every little brother's goal their whole life is to beat their big brother at something. Those were interesting games when I started getting bigger."[113]

Stockton's small size also meant that he was pushed around during neighborhood pickup games. The physical pressure only strengthened his determination to play better:

John Stockton's tenaciousness in playing the game was started by him playing with his older brother.

I remember when I was in sixth or seventh grade, and I came home crying, my father said, "Maybe you shouldn't play with those boys, maybe they're too rough." He said it in a kindly way, but it made me take it as a challenge. Maybe I was stupid, but I went back out to show them I could play.[114]

Catholic Education

Stockton always attended Catholic schools, and he was a sports standout at each one. Basketball was not his only talent. During elementary school at St. Aloysius, he set a city grade-school record for the mile run.

The young athlete knew that practice and hard work were the keys to becoming a successful basketball player. Since he was not as big as the other kids, he found other ways to be better, such as improving his passing, dribbling, and defensive skills. It was not unusual for Stockton to arrive at school at 6:00 A.M., just to get in some extra practice with his basketball coach.

When Stockton enrolled at Gonzaga Prep High School in 1976, he was only five feet, five inches tall and weighed only ninety pounds. Despite his small size, he soon won a starting position as point guard for the basketball team.

Even though Stockton was a good player—once scoring 42 points in a game—no one expected he would ever be good enough, or big enough, to play professionally. "The only person in the world who thought John would play in the NBA was John,"[115] his father once said.

Stockton knew that size was not the most important thing in the NBA. His hero was pro basketball player Gus Williams, who was barely over six feet tall and played for the Seattle Supersonics. If Williams could do it, Stockton figured, he could too.

Although Stockton had big basketball dreams, he did not want to be a show-off. "During high school, he wouldn't even let his parents buy him a letter jacket. In fact, he never wore anything that would let people know he was an athlete,"[116] writes basketball commentator Phil Taylor.

Small College, Big Player

Stockton graduated from Gonzaga Prep in 1980 and went on to Gonzaga University in his hometown of Spokane. Today, Gonzaga is nationally known in the NCAA, but in 1980, it was not a big name in college basketball. However, Stockton had played many pickup games in Gonzaga's gym, and he liked the idea of staying in his hometown and attending the same college his father had.

Attending a small college gave Stockton a chance to shine as a basketball player. Although he did not get much playing time as a freshman, he made the starting lineup during his sophomore year and got to play in almost every game. Logging so much playing time allowed Stockton to learn how to handle skilled opponents by actually being on the court with them, not just watching from the bench. At six feet, one inch tall and 175 pounds, Stockton was still smaller than most of the other players on the court. However, Stockton thrived in his underdog role and worked especially hard to make his presence felt.

Stockton's average got better every year he played. During his sophomore year, he scored an average of 11.2 points and 5 assists per game. By his junior year, Stockton was up to almost 14 points and 7 assists per game. During his senior year, Stockton had his best season, averaging almost 21 points and more than 7 assists per game. Those averages were the best in the West Coast Athletic Conference and won Stockton the league's MVP title for the

1983–1984 season. He was also considered to be one of the nation's best collegiate point guards.

In 1984, Stockton was invited to try out for the U.S. Olympic team, which would play in Los Angeles that summer. Stockton impressed everyone with his hard work and skill and won the attention of some NBA scouts who had come to watch the tryouts. Stockton almost made the team, but ended up being one of the last players cut from the team. Although he was disappointed, Stockton felt he had proven himself among the best amateur players in the country. "Deep inside he knew he was as good as most of the players there," his brother, Steve, noted. "It was like a springboard."[117] That springboard would take Stockton right into the NBA.

The Utah Jazz stunned many people by selecting Stockton in the first round of the 1984 NBA draft.

Into the Pros

After his performance in the Olympic tryouts, there was strong interest in Stockton from NBA scouts. For the first time, many people took him seriously as a player who had professional potential. Still, many people did not think that Stockton would be picked in the NBA draft in 1984, because the draft included many more well-known players, such as Michael Jordan, Hakeem Olajuwon, and Charles Barkley.

The Utah Jazz had their eye on Stockton, though, and surprised many people by picking him in the first round of the draft. Jazz fans were not upset with the choice, just surprised. Most of them had never heard of John Stockton.

Stockton kept busy during the months between the draft and the day he reported to practice. He studied videos of the Jazz players to learn their style of play. By the time he joined the team, he knew exactly how the players worked and what kind of ball they played.

Stockton spent most of his first two seasons on the bench as a backup to longtime Jazz guards Darrell Griffith and Rickey Green. When he did play, Stockton made the most of his time on the court, setting up plays and passing the ball for his teammates to score.

A New Teammate

In 1985, the Jazz selected forward Karl Malone in the NBA draft. In many ways, Malone was the opposite of Stockton. While Stockton was white, small, and quiet, Malone was black, big, and loud. But despite their differences, the two soon became an unbeatable team.

Karl Malone has called Stockton "the smartest player I have ever played with."[118] The two worked together beautifully. Stockton would pass Malone the ball, and Malone would score. At the same time, Malone protected Stockton from larger, more aggressive players on the court. Their partnership was the start of a new era for the Jazz. The two were such a solid team that, when he was named MVP of the 1989 All-Star Game, Malone said, "I would have to split this award right down the middle and give half of it to John."[119]

During the 1987–1988 season, Stockton finally became the Jazz's starting point guard, replacing the injured Rickey Green. Soon he was one of the best point guards in the NBA. That season, Stockton set a new single-season record of 1,128 assists and became

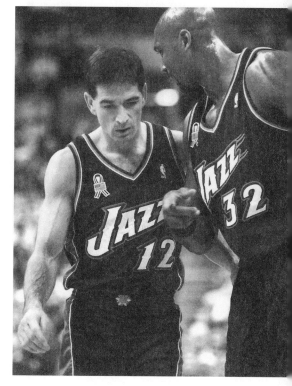

Stockton and Karl Malone plan their offense against the Celtics during a game in December 2001. The two made a dynamic team.

one of only three players to score more than 1,000 assists in one season. "I will come around off a pick and in the split-second I am open, the ball will just be sitting there, waiting to be a shot,"[120] said Stockton's teammate, Jeff Hornacek.

Stockton also had a knack for stealing the ball and was ranked third in the league that season. "You can't relax for a second with him," complained point guard Johnny Dawkins, who played for several NBA teams, including the San Antonio Spurs and the Philadelphia 76ers. "He sees everything and he is aware of everything."[121]

Another Magic?

Many people compared Stockton to another famous playmaker, Magic Johnson. Former coach K.C. Jones once said that Stockton was "a small Magic Johnson. He always seems to make the right decision at the right time."[122]

Stockton and Johnson had the chance to face off against each other during the 1988 NBA semifinals, when the Jazz played the Lakers. The Lakers dominated the Jazz and won the first game, but the Jazz took the next two games. Fans were thrilled to watch Stockton in action against Johnson. The results could be surprising. During the fourth quarter of the third game, Stockton was so dominant that Johnson actually retreated to the bench.

Despite the excellent play of Stockton and Malone, the Jazz lost to the Los Angeles Lakers in seven games. But Stockton came away with a new record—115 assists in the series. The previous holder of that record had been none other than Magic Johnson. Johnson himself had high praise for the smaller, younger guard. He said, "There's nobody who can distribute the ball plus lead his team like John Stockton."[123]

Although there would be more play-off appearances for the Jazz, and they would play in several NBA finals, the team would never win a championship. Despite his disappointment, Stockton looked at the bright side. "I'd like to win one, but if that's the only way you can put a positive value on yourself, then you're in big trouble."[124]

However, Stockton continued racking up personal triumphs. He led the league in assists every year between 1988 and 1996. By the beginning of the 2001 season, he had a staggering 14,503 assists. Stockton was also named one of the 50 Greatest Players in NBA History in 1996. "John can let guys cross and cut through and, all of a sudden, bang, something happens for him," said Utah coach Jerry Sloan. "From that standpoint, I'd say he's probably the best I've ever seen."[125]

Stockton passes the ball at the game where he received his 15,000th career assist.

Olympic Dreams

Stockton had failed to make the Olympic team in 1984. Things would be different in 1992, when the Summer Olympics were held in Barcelona, Spain. For the first time, professional athletes were allowed to represent the sport. The U.S. team was made up of the brightest stars of the NBA, including Magic Johnson, Michael Jordan, Charles Barkley, and Karl Malone. Although Stockton had excellent stats, many fans were surprised and even angry that he had been chosen. They thought that guard Isiah Thomas of the Detroit Pistons deserved the honor more, because he had led the Pistons to NBA championships in 1989 and 1990.

Stockton refused to get involved in the controversy over his selection. Unfortunately, he suffered a broken leg during one of the qualifying games and was unable to play in the finals. However, the team went on to win a gold medal. Stockton also played on the gold medal–winning Olympic basketball team in the 1996 Olympics in Atlanta.

All-Star Controversies

Stockton shone during the 1993 All-Star Game, which was played on the Jazz's home court in Salt Lake City, Utah. Once again, the team of Stockton and Malone stole the show. Malone scored 28 points and Stockton had 15 assists. Their performances led to them being named co-MVPs of the game.

"We had a saying in high school and college, 'Make your teammate an All-American,' and in this case, 'Make your teammate an All-Star,' and Stock is one of those guys," Malone once said. "He always tries to go out and make his teammates All-Stars. People ask me what I would be without him, and I don't even want to think about it."[126]

However, Stockton's All-Star experiences were not always positive. Because of his low profile, he rarely received enough votes to be named to the team, although the NBA coaches usually ensured that he had a backup place on the squad. Karl Malone, on the other hand, almost always won a spot on the team during the 1990s. In 1998, Malone received more votes than anybody else in the Western Conference, which meant he would be a starter. However, Stockton was not voted in by the fans or the coaches, since he had missed eighteen games because of an injury.

Malone was so angry about his friend's absence that he threatened to boycott the All-Star Game. In the end, he did play, but admitted, "It's weird. It's definitely weird that he's not here. . . . It's unfortunate; considering what he does for our team and what he does for the game, I think he should be here."[127] As usual, however, Stockton did not complain.

A Quiet Hero

Stockton continues to play excellent basketball into the early years of the twenty-first century. In 2001, the Jazz signed him to a two-year, $18 million contract.

Despite his success, Stockton remains quiet and unassuming. Phil Taylor writes:

Watch him as he leaves. The buzzer sounds, and by the time your eye finds him, he's already in the tunnel leading to the locker room, like a base stealer who has gotten a good jump. He's walking swiftly, taking long, purposeful strides, as though he has just remembered something elsewhere that requires his immediate attention. The eyes that moments earlier were darting, taking in every movement on the court as he directed the Utah Jazz attack, are now staring straight ahead, meeting no one's gaze. The game is over, so there's nothing left here for John Stockton, nothing that interests him in the least. The court is filling with peripheral people—photographers, sideline TV reporters, nameless folk with credentials around their necks and no function he remotely cares about. Stockton is a man at a party who realizes it's not his kind of crowd.[128]

Despite his tremendous basketball successes, Stockton remains a quiet and unassuming NBA superstar.

"Some people think John's cold, but he's not," explained his teammate, forward Thurl Bailey.

It's just that if he could take away all the accolades, all the hoopla, all the nationally televised interviews and just play basketball, he'd be in heaven. John might be the one player who really wouldn't miss it if the fame went away tomorrow and all he was left with was the game.[129]

Stockton has always been more interested in being a team player who helps the Jazz win than in performing flashy moves that draw attention to himself. "I think I saw him go behind the back against Bobby Hurley once, a couple of years ago," said one of his teammates. "That's about as Showtime as John gets."[130]

Stockton extends his no-frills style to his personal life. He married his college sweetheart, has five children, and lives next door to his parents' house in Spokane. This might not be the style of other NBA stars, but it is just right for Stockton. "You don't do anything just because other people do," he once said. "My father taught me that."[131]

When he is not playing for the Jazz, Stockton spends much of his time working out in the gym at Gonzaga University, where he went to college. He knows there is one big reason for his success. "It might sound boring, but it comes from hard work. The only way to make it in anything is hard work. You have to do what you're told, listen and learn, but without hard work, you'll have a tough time having success."[132]

CHAPTER 6

Michael Jordan:
The Greatest Ever

Many basketball players have been called great. But one player towers above them all, in terms of his athletic ability, his outstanding career, and his celebrity. That player is Michael Jordan, who may well be the greatest basketball player in history. His fame transcended the sport, making him one of the most recognizable figures in the world.

Humble Beginnings

Michael Jeffrey Jordan was born on February 17, 1963, in the New York City borough of Brooklyn. When Jordan was still very young, his parents became concerned about raising a family in the city. They decided that life would be better for Jordan and his brothers and sisters if they lived away from the constant street violence and drug dealing that plagued their Brooklyn neighborhood. So the family moved to the small, quiet town of Wilmington, North Carolina.

Jordan's parents gave their children a sense of dedication and hard work. "It was always like that in our family," Jordan's father, James, once said. "We always tried to make things happen rather than wait around for them to happen. And we've always found that if you work hard, you can make it happen."[133]

Like many boys his age, Jordan loved to play sports. As a child, his favorite sport was baseball. He and his father spent many hours tossing a baseball back and forth. Jordan was also an important member of Wilmington's Babe Ruth League team. He played in the outfield and also pitched. When he was twelve years old, he was named the league's best player after he helped Wilmington win the state baseball championship.

Jordan also played basketball, but he was not very good at it at first. He usually played with his older brother, Larry. Even though Larry was only five feet, seven inches tall, he regularly beat his younger brother in one-on-one games. None of the men in the

Jordan family was over six feet tall, and Jordan himself did not think he would be tall enough to seriously compete in the sport.

Not Good Enough

Even though he was not tall or especially good at basketball, Jordan liked to play. When he enrolled at Wilmington's Laney High School, he tried out for the varsity team. However, the coach, Clifton "Pop" Herring, did not think Jordan was good enough. Instead, the five-foot-ten-inch-tall Jordan played on the junior varsity team. He did well, averaging 25 points a game.

During his sophomore year, Laney High School's basketball team went to the play-offs. The team needed an extra player, and Jordan was sure he would be chosen. However, the varsity took one of his taller teammates on the junior varsity team. Jordan was disappointed, but he became excited when his team moved on to the regionals.

Michael Jordan dunks a basket at Laney High School. Jordan was not nationally famous as a high school player, unlike many other stars.

Jordan longed to be part of the team, but he was allowed to go to the regionals only because a student manager got sick. Instead of playing, Jordan carried uniforms, then sat on the bench handing out towels to the other players as they came off the court. Jordan found the experience humiliating. "I made up my mind there that this would never happen to me again," Jordan later said. "From that point on, I started working harder than ever on my basketball skills."[134]

That summer, Jordan attended basketball camps and spent hours practicing shots at home, both alone and with his brother. He also grew five inches to six feet, three inches in height. By the time school started again in September, Jordan was ready for the varsity team.

The Tar Heels

Jordan performed well on the varsity. It was clear he was becoming a real basketball talent. Even so, he was not nationally known as a high school star, like many other NBA sensations. Looking back, Jordan considers this a good thing. "I never had any of that notoriety in high school and that was probably a blessing because I always had the hunger. I was never compared with the greatest of all time, and I didn't burn out early as a result."[135]

During the summer before his senior year of high school, Jordan attended the Five-Star Basketball Camp. At the camp,

Jordan reaches high to overcome a block during a game for the University of North Carolina.

Jordan met Dean Smith, the legendary coach of the University of North Carolina's Tar Heels. The Tar Heels were one of the best college basketball teams in the country. Smith saw Jordan's potential and talked to him about attending the University of North Carolina (UNC). A few months later, Jordan signed a letter of intent to attend the school and received a full scholarship.

Jordan's senior year at Laney High School was a basketball triumph. He led the team to 19 wins. When he graduated in June 1981, he was more than ready to play college ball.

It was very rare for a freshman to win a spot on UNC's varsity team under Coach Dean Smith. Before Jordan enrolled at the school, only three freshmen had done it. Jordan became the fourth. Although he spent most of the season as a backup player and not a starter, Jordan did have an impact on the team during an important game.

The Tar Heels had an outstanding season and went on to play in the 1982 NCAA Championship against Georgetown University. With only two seconds left to play, Georgetown was leading by one point. Then Jordan grabbed the ball and made a last-second jump shot. The ball went in, and the Tar Heels won the national championship. Suddenly, basketball fans around the country were talking about Michael Jordan.

Jordan played with the Tar Heels for two more seasons, and averaged a respectable 17.7 points per game. He was also named to the All-American team and named Player of the Year as a sophomore and junior.

Jordan's college teammates remember him as fiercely competitive. "Michael just dominated," said Matt Doherty. "His intensity was high, he was taking the ball to the basket, dunking on these guys, not showing these veterans any respect. That just opened your eyes and made you realize he was special."[136]

Sportswriter Mitchell Krugel also recalled Jordan's intensity:

> Even before starting college, Jordan demonstrated star qualities. Certain plays he made and the way he went about trying to improve his abilities provided proof that MJ was going to be a player who could do what no one had done before. There were those who, after their first up-close look at Michael, knew he was going to be one of the all-time greats.[137]

After his junior year, Jordan felt he was ready for the NBA. After announcing his decision to turn pro, he was picked third in the 1984 NBA draft. Jordan was chosen by the Chicago Bulls, a team with one of the worst records in the league. Sportswriter Brad Herzog recalled, "Before Jordan, Chicago had difficulty filling one-third of Chicago Stadium, averaging just over 6,000 spectators per home game."[138] The Bulls were the laughingstock of the sports world. But all that was about to change.

Feeling Bullish

Before he joined the Bulls for the 1984–1985 season, Jordan traveled to Los Angeles as part of the U.S. Olympic basketball team. Jordan scored an average of 17 points per game and helped the team to win a gold medal. Then, it was off to Chicago. An amazing career was about to begin.

From the start, Jordan was a standout for the Bulls. Even during practice, he played with a white-hot intensity, trying to make every shot or block on every play. Teammate Orlando Woolridge recalled, "He was so much quicker than any of us, and he could jump so much higher. He made the game seem really easy. But that wasn't what was special about Michael. I never saw anybody compete like that. He competed every day. He approached every practice like it was a game, like it was *the* game."[139]

During his first season, Jordan led the team in points, rebounds, assists, and steals, and had no trouble winning the Rookie of the Year award. He was also named to the All-Star Team. And the Chicago Bulls, who were once so bad that hardly anyone went to their games, made it all the way to the first round of the NBA play-offs.

Personal Bests

Although he was sidelined for most of the 1985–1986 season with a broken foot, Jordan returned in time for the play-offs. During one game, he scored an incredible 63 points, setting a play-off scoring record.

Jordan was also an excellent defensive player. "I think Michael was one of the most feared defenders in the league," said his coach, Phil Jackson. "I say feared because most everybody wasn't aware of where he was on the floor and what he was doing. He could make a block or get a steal and the whole game would change."[140] Teammate Darrell Walker put it more simply: "Anytime Michael wanted to get between his man and the bucket and shut him off, he could."[141]

Despite Jordan's awesome abilities, he could not carry an entire team. In 1986, the Bulls lost before reaching the finals. The same thing would happen for the next five seasons.

Jordan dominates a 1988 game. That year he received his first NBA Most Valuable Player award.

Although the Bulls did not make it to the championships, Jordan was setting many records of his own. During the 1986–1987 season, it was not unusual for him to score more than 50 points a game. He ended that season with 3,041 points. Jordan was only the second player to score more than 3,000 points in a single season. The first player to achieve this milestone was Wilt Chamberlain. Jordan also won his first of seven straight scoring titles.

Unfortunately, Jordan was almost *too* good. He dominated the other players so much that the Bulls could not function as a team. As a result, they often lost to other teams who worked as a unit. The Bulls also went through several coaches who were not able to integrate the players into a team.

Then, in 1988, Phil Jackson was promoted from assistant coach to head coach of the Bulls. He realized that Jordan could not carry the team by himself if they expected to win a championship. Jackson created a new offensive strategy that did not rely on Jordan alone. Instead, he teamed Jordan with two new Bulls players, Scottie Pippen and Horace Grant.

The results were electrifying. Jordan, Pippen, and Grant brought out the best in each other and worked as a unit to score. Jackson was able to build plays around these players and crafted a creative and aggressive strategy that overwhelmed opponents.

Champions!

The hard work of Jackson and his team finally paid off in 1991, when the Bulls won their first championship. The victory was sweet, but the team was only getting started.

From 1991 to 1993, the Bulls won three straight championships. Jordan was named MVP in 1991 and 1992. Jordan also won seven consecutive scoring titles. Between 1988 and 1993, he scored more than 60 points in a game five times and scored more than 50 points almost thirty-six times. He also found time to lead the U.S. Olympic team to a gold medal at the 1992 Olympics in Barcelona, Spain.

Jordan became a worldwide superstar. "I want to be like Mike" became a refrain heard in every schoolyard. "On the play-grounds, young boys all over the world have tried to emulate his

Sailing above the ground, Jordan dunks a ball for a Nike advertisement. With his gravity-defying style, Jordan became a cultural icon.

high-flying, gravity-defying style. Jordan became a cultural icon unlike any athlete in history,"[142] wrote Herzog.

"The only person in my lifetime I can compare to Michael is Elvis Presley," said the Bulls' owner, Jerry Reinsdorf. "He wasn't just a singer, and Michael isn't just an athlete. They are cult figures, bigger than life."[143]

Jordan's charisma was a big part of his appeal. He was handsome and had a warm, friendly smile and a wonderful sense of style. Most of all, he had a vertical jump that seemed to defy gravity. "I've never had my vertical leap measured, but sometimes I think about how high I get up," Jordan once said. "I always spread my legs when I jump high, and it seems like I've opened a parachute that slowly brings me back to the floor."[144]

Sportswriter Mitchell Krugel tried to explain Jordan's amazing leaps. "What made his jump unique was what came *after* he left the ground. Jordan was the one player who could leap and gain momentum while in the air. Gravity would naturally bring a player back to the ground. But not Jordan. . . . Michael's bunny-hop gave him extra spring, off which he could twist sideways and slip defenders in midair."[145] Jordan's ability to literally float up to the basket gave him a new nickname: Air Jordan.

Jordan never let his superstar status prevent him from working hard at the game. He remained fiercely competitive and dedicated to keeping his skills at their top level. "Always know there is someone out there striving to be a better player than you," he told fans in an online interview with CBS Sportsline. "That means you must always strive to stay ahead of the next player."[146]

Tragedy and Change

In the summer of 1993, Jordan received horrifying news. His father, James Jordan, had been murdered at a highway rest stop by two young men in North Carolina.

Jordan was devastated by the loss of his father. "I think about him every day," he told journalist Bob Greene. "Every single day. I think about him when I'm worried, and I think about him when I have a decision to make. I think about him when I have a bad problem. I think about what advice he would give me, what he would say to me. . . . He's with me."[147]

His father's murder was the biggest tragedy of Michael's life, and it made him change his priorities. Suddenly, playing basketball did not seem that important anymore. Jordan felt he had achieved all he could on the basketball court. His father's death reminded him that life was short, and if he wanted to try something new, now was the time. As Bulls' owner Jerry Reinsdorf put it, "It came to a point where there was no more return on investment. It wasn't worth it anymore."[148] Two months after James Jordan died, his son retired from basketball.

Jordan decided to turn his energies to a different sport. Despite his phenomenal success on the basketball court, he had always harbored a dream to be a professional baseball player. Now he decided it was time to make that dream a reality.

When Jordan announced his decision to the public, he was met with disbelief and even ridicule. As Greene explains, "Many fans and sports experts . . . were scoffing at the idea of what he

Two months after the murder of his father James (pictured), Jordan decided to retire from basketball.

was about to try. As skilled as he was at playing basketball, they said, he would be unable to master hitting big-league fastballs and curves. All he was about to do, these people said, was to humiliate himself in public."[149]

Jordan's response was confident and unapologetic. "I love to hear them say that," he said. "My whole life, that's been the kind of thing that has driven me. You tell me that I can't do something, and I'm going to do it."[150]

Jordan was quickly signed by the Chicago White Sox. After workouts at Chicago's Comiskey Park, he began his baseball career as an outfielder with the Birmingham Barons of the Southern League, one of Chicago's minor league teams. Jordan worked as hard at playing baseball as he did at basketball. But although he was a reliable player, with a .202 average, 51 runs batted in, 3 home runs, and 30 stolen bases, it soon became clear that he was not able to compete with major league talent.

In the spring of 1995, major league baseball players went out on a strike that shortened the season. Although Jordan was offered a position with the White Sox as a replacement player in the majors, he declined. Instead, he ended his baseball career.

Even though he was not as successful as he had hoped to be, Jordan did not regret his baseball experiment:

> I could never be so perfect that no one could ever find something bad to say about me. And my only answer was to decide: OK, I'm going to do the best I can. But I'm human. Do I have flaws? Have I made mistakes, and will

Jordan takes a swing for the Chicago White Sox during the 1994 Crosstown Classic against the Cubs. A day later he made his debut with the Birmingham Barons.

I make mistakes? Yep, I have and I will. So here I am, this time around—a human being. Before, every second of every day was devoted to living up to a certain image. Every second was built around being afraid of doing something that would destroy me. I'm not going to be afraid anymore. I can only do my best. I'm not going to be afraid that someone will find out when I've failed.[151]

Jordan also said, "There's only one person who can tell you whether you've won or lost. And that's you."[152]

When Jordan announced that he would return to basketball, Bulls fans were delirious with happiness. The team had struggled to win without Jordan, but now things were looking up. Posters of Jordan playing basketball appeared around Chicago, announcing "The Second Coming."

On Top of the World Again

When Jordan rejoined the Bulls, there were only seventeen games left in the season. Although the team made it to the play-offs, they were defeated by the Orlando Magic.

The 1995–1996 season was a different story. Although Jordan was no longer "a young whiz in his twenties,"[153] as Bob Greene described him, he was still one of the best players in the game. Under his leadership, and joined by powerful players such as Scottie Pippen, Dennis Rodman, and Toni Kukoc, the Bulls roared to a record-breaking 72-10 season. Then they went on to win the NBA championship. Jordan was named Most Valuable Player of the regular season and the championship series. He was the first player to win the championship MVP award four times.

Jordan and the Bulls were not finished yet. In the 1996–1997 season, the Bulls had a 69-13 record and Jordan led the league in scoring, with an average of almost 30 points a game. The Bulls won the championship again, and Jordan notched his fifth MVP award. The 1997–1998 season saw Jordan leading the league again with almost 29 points per game. The Bulls had a 62-20 record, won their sixth championship, and saw Jordan win his sixth NBA Finals MVP award.

Time for a Change

After the 1998 season, Phil Jackson left the Bulls to coach the Los Angeles Lakers. Jordan was not interested in playing for another coach or another team. There also seemed to be little left to accomplish in basketball. So, in January 1999, Jordan once again

announced his retirement from professional basketball. When he left, he had a career total of 29,277 points, 5,836 rebounds, 5,012 assists, and 2,036 steals. He also held the record for the highest career scoring average with 31.5 points a game and led the league in scoring a record ten seasons.

Basketball continued to attract Jordan. He went on to become part-owner of the basketball team the Washington Wizards. In 2001, he surprised everyone by giving up his stake in the team to play for them.

However, Jordan's second comeback has not been as dramatic as his first. The Wizards have not dominated the NBA the way the Bulls did during the 1990s. Jordan himself can no longer score 50 points a night or dazzle opponents and fans with his unbelievable moves. However, he played well and enjoyed a more low-profile career for several months, without the pressures he faced while playing for the Bulls or attempting a baseball career.

Jordan's body was not up to the challenge of professional basketball, however, and he left the team early in 2002 to undergo knee surgery, his continuing professional basketball career uncertain.

Jordan enthralls a crowd of shouting onlookers as he makes the winning shot in Game 6 of the 1998 NBA Finals.

A Shining Legacy

Michael Jordan forever changed not only basketball but the role of athletes in popular culture. More than a sports figure, he be-

A Filipino youth gazes at posters of Jordan being sold along a sidewalk in a commercial center in Manila. Jordan's fame reaches across the globe.

came a cultural icon and one of the most recognized people in the world. His basketball career led to a number of product endorsements, including his own line of Nike shoes, called Air Jordans. He also owns a chain of restaurants named after him.

Jordan's appeal transcended race, and he became, according to Brad Herzog, "the marketing world's first truly successful crossover athlete, an African American beloved by blacks and whites alike."[154] *Sports Illustrated* writer E.M. Swift explained, "Until Jordan arrived on the scene, only a handful of African American athletes were able to parlay their multicultural popularity into anything more bankable than good will."[155]

Jordan also receives credit for bringing basketball and the NBA to new heights of popularity. Herzog writes,

> When all is said and done, Jordan's most enduring legacy is not about dollars and cents, but about the game of basketball. The Jordan image led to a cavalcade of individual stars in the NBA and spurred the league to places where only the NFL and Major League Baseball once ruled supreme.[156]

Today, many athletes feel there is no greater compliment than to be called the next Michael Jordan. Jordan himself dislikes these comparisons. He told Greene:

> There's a person out there who's going to be great. . . . We don't know who he is yet. But whoever he is . . . no one's doing him any favor by comparing him to me. When the person comes along, and he's the real thing, you'll know it because he'll be so good that no one compares him to anyone else.[157]

In the world of basketball, there is always another great athlete ready to take the ball and run with it.

NOTES

Chapter 1: George Mikan: The Big Man

1. Quoted in Brad Herzog, *The Sports 100*. New York: Macmillan, 1995, p. 208.

2. Quoted in *Sports Trivia*, "George Mikan 1924– ," www.sports-trivia.net.

3. Quoted in Ron Fimrite, "Big George," *Sports Illustrated*, November 6, 1989, p. 136.

4. Quoted in Herzog, *The Sports 100*, p. 209.

5. Quoted in Herzog, *The Sports 100*, p. 209.

6. Quoted in Herzog, *The Sports 100*, p. 209.

7. Quoted in Fimrite, "Big George," p. 136.

8. Quoted in *Sports Trivia*, "George Mikan 1924– ."

9. Quoted in Ira Berkow, "Mikan Ruled an Era, and Changed the Rules," *New York Times*, March 11, 2001, sect. 8, p. 11.

10. Quoted in Fimrite, "Big George," p. 136.

11. Quoted in Herzog, *The Sports 100*, p. 210.

12. Quoted in Dave Anderson, *The Story of Basketball*. New York: William Morrow, 1988, p. 46.

13. Quoted in Herzog, *The Sports 100*, p. 210.

14. Quoted in Berkow, "Mikan Ruled an Era, and Changed the Rules," p. 11.

15. Quoted in Berkow, "Mikan Ruled an Era, and Changed the Rules," p. 11.

16. Quoted in *Sports Trivia*, "George Mikan 1924– ."

17. Quoted in Ira Berkow, "Mikan Makes a Comeback," *New York Times*, March 26, 1997, p. B13.

18. Quoted in Fimrite, "Big George," p. 139.

19. Quoted in Kelli Anderson, "George Mikan," *Sports Illustrated*, August 22, 1994, p. 52.

20. *Sports Trivia*, "George Mikan 1924– ."

21. Quoted in Kevin and Laurie Hillstrom, "Wilt Chamberlain," *Biography Today Sports Series,* vol. 4. Detroit: Omnigraphics, 2000, p. 10.

22. Wilt Chamberlain, *A View from Above.* New York: Villard Books, 1991, p. 27.

23. Quoted in Hillstrom, "Wilt Chamberlain," p. 10.

24. Chamberlain, *A View from Above,* p. 11.

25. Chamberlain, *A View from Above,* pp. 11–12.

26. Quoted in Hillstrom, "Wilt Chamberlain," pp. 10–11.

27. Quoted in George Sullivan, *Great Lives: Sports.* New York: Charles Scribner's Sons, 1988, p. 41.

28. Chamberlain, *A View from Above,* p. 149.

29. Wilt Chamberlain, *Wilt: Just Like Any Other 7-Foot Black Millionaire Who Lives Next Door.* New York: Macmillan, 1973, p. 51.

30. Chamberlain, *Wilt,* pp. 56–57.

31. Quoted in Sullivan, *Great Lives: Sports,* p. 42.

32. Chamberlain, *Wilt,* p. 83.

33. Quoted in Sullivan, *Great Lives: Sports,* p. 42.

34. Quoted in Hillstrom, "Wilt Chamberlain," p. 14.

35. Quoted in Hillstrom, "Wilt Chamberlain," p. 14.

36. Quoted in Hillstrom, "Wilt Chamberlain," p. 15.

37. Quoted in Sullivan, *Great Lives: Sports,* p. 43.

38. Quoted in Anderson, *The Story of Basketball,* p. 56.

39. Quoted in Sullivan, *Great Lives: Sports,* 1988, p. 47.

40. Quoted in Anderson, *The Story of Basketball,* p. 56.

41. Quoted in Anderson, *The Story of Basketball,* p. 57.

42. Quoted in Hillstrom, "Wilt Chamberlain," p. 18.

43. Quoted in Hillstrom, "Wilt Chamberlain," p. 18.

44. Quoted in Hillstrom, "Wilt Chamberlain," p. 18.

45. Quoted in Hillstrom, "Wilt Chamberlain," p. 19.

46. Quoted in Hillstrom, "Wilt Chamberlain," p. 20.

47. Chamberlain, *Wilt,* p. 302.

48. Quoted in Hillstrom, "Wilt Chamberlain," p. 18.

49. Chamberlain, *A View from Above,* p. 26.

50. Quoted in Hillstrom, "Wilt Chamberlain," p. 22.

51. Quoted in Hillstrom, "Wilt Chamberlain," p. 22.

Chapter 3: Kareem Abdul-Jabbar: Scoring Champion

52. Quoted in Kevin and Laurie Hillstrom, "Kareem Abdul-Jabbar," *Biography Today Sports Series,* vol. 1. Detroit: Omnigraphics, 1996, p. 21.

53. Kareem Abdul-Jabbar, *Giant Steps.* New York: Bantam Books, 1983, p. 15.

54. Quoted in Hillstrom, "Kareem Abdul-Jabbar," p. 21.

55. Abdul-Jabbar, *Giant Steps,* p. 24.

56. Abdul-Jabbar, *Giant Steps,* p. 25.

57. Quoted in Anderson, *The Story of Basketball.* p. 100.

58. Abdul-Jabbar, *Giant Steps,* p. 34.

59. Quoted in Hillstrom, "Kareem Abdul-Jabbar," p. 22.

60. Abdul-Jabbar, *Giant Steps,* p. 69.

61. Abdul-Jabbar, *Giant Steps,* p. 72.

62. Quoted in Hillstrom, "Kareem Abdul-Jabbar," pp. 22–23.

63. Abdul-Jabbar, *Giant Steps,* p. 105.

64. Quoted in Anderson, *The Story of Basketball,* p. 73.

65. Quoted in Hillstrom, "Kareem Abdul-Jabbar," pp. 23–24.

66. Abdul-Jabbar, *Giant Steps,* p. 166.

67. Quoted in Hillstrom, "Kareem Abdul-Jabbar," p. 24.

68. Abdul-Jabbar, *Giant Steps,* p. 230.

69. Abdul-Jabbar, *Giant Steps,* p. 233.

70. Abdul-Jabbar, *Giant Steps,* pp. 280–281.

71. Abdul-Jabbar, *Giant Steps,* p. 266.

72. Abdul-Jabbar, *Giant Steps,* pp. 283–84.

73. Abdul-Jabbar, *Giant Steps,* p. 285.

74. Abdul-Jabbar, *Giant Steps,* p. 306.

75. Quoted in Hillstrom, "Kareem Abdul-Jabbar," p. 26.

76. Quoted in Joe Garner, *And the Fans Roared.* Naperville, IL: Sourcebooks, 2000, p. 81.

77. Quoted in Hillstrom, "Kareem Abdul-Jabbar," p. 26.

78. Abdul-Jabbar, *Giant Steps,* p. 320.

79. Quoted in Hillstrom, "Kareem Abdul-Jabbar," p. 28.

80. Quoted in Hillstrom, "Kareem Abdul-Jabbar," p. 28.

Chapter 4: Magic Johnson: Making Things Happen

81. Earvin "Magic" Johnson, *My Life.* New York: Random House, 1992, p. 3.

82. Johnson, *My Life,* p. 11.

83. Johnson, *My Life,* p. 14.

84. Johnson, *My Life,* pp. 21–22.

85. Johnson, *My Life,* p. 24.

86. Johnson, *My Life,* p. 27.

87. Johnson, *My Life,* p. 31.

88. Johnson, *My Life,* p. 29.

89. Quoted in Anderson, *The Story of Basketball,* p. 83.

90. Johnson, *My Life,* p. 73.

91. Herzog, *The Sports 100,* p. 149.

92. Quoted in Herzog, *The Sports 100,* p. 149.

93. Johnson, *My Life,* p. 88.

94. Johnson, *My Life,* p. 101.

95. Anderson, *The Story of Basketball,* p. 83.

96. Quoted in Anderson, *The Story of Basketball,* p. 85.

97. Quoted in Johnson, *My Life,* p. 112.

98. Quoted in Herzog, *The Sports 100,* p. 150.

99. Quoted in Anderson, *The Story of Basketball,* p. 121.

100. Quoted in Anderson, *The Story of Basketball,* pp. 121–22.

101. Johnson, *My Life,* p. 236.

102. Johnson, *My Life,* pp. 262–63

103. Johnson, *My Life,* p. 267.

104. Quoted in Herzog, *The Sports 100*, p. 151.

105. Jack McCallum, "Pure Magic," *Reader's Digest*, May 2002, p. 133.

106. Quoted in Herzog, *The Sports 100*, p. 151.

107. Quoted in Herzog, *The Sports 100*, p. 151.

108. Johnson, *My Life*, p. 308.

109. Quoted in Herzog, *The Sports 100*, p. 152.

110. Quoted in McCallum, "Pure Magic," *Reader's Digest*, p. 134.

111. Johnson, *My Life*, p. 329.

Chapter 5: John Stockton: A True Team Player

112. Quoted in Phil Taylor, "Keep It Simple," *JazzHoops.com*. http://jazzhoops.net.

113. Quoted in Kevin and Lauri Hillstrom, "John Stockton," *Biography Today Sports Series*, vol. 3. Detroit: Omnigraphics, 1999 p. 125.

114. Quoted in Hillstrom, "John Stockton," p. 125.

115. Quoted in Hillstrom, "John Stockton," p. 125.

116. Taylor, "Keep It Simple."

117. Quoted in Hillstrom, "John Stockton," p. 126.

118. Quoted in Oren and Saar Haas, *The Ultimate John Stockton Page*. www.geocities.com.

119. Quoted in Haas, *The Ultimate John Stockton Page*.

120. Quoted in Haas, *The Ultimate John Stockton Page*.

121. Quoted in Haas, *The Ultimate John Stockton Page*.

122. Quoted in Haas, *The Ultimate John Stockton Page*.

123. Quoted in Haas, *The Ultimate John Stockton Page*.

124. Quoted in Hillstrom, "John Stockton," p. 131.

125. Quoted in Hillstrom, "John Stockton," p. 127.

126. Quoted in *Current Biography Excerpts*, "Basketball," 1996, www.hwwilson.com.

127. Quoted in Michael Lewis, *To the Brink: Stockton, Malone, and the Utah Jazz's Climb to the Edge of Glory*. New York: Simon & Schuster, 1998, p. 135.

128. Taylor, "Keep It Simple."

129. Quoted in Taylor, "Keep It Simple."

130. Quoted in Taylor, "Keep It Simple."

131. Quoted in Taylor, "Keep It Simple."

132. Quoted in Hillstrom, "John Stockton," p. 127.

Chapter 6: Michael Jordan: The Greatest Ever

133. Quoted in *Michael Jordan Biography.* www.geocities.com.

134. Quoted in *Michael Jordan Biography.*

135. Quoted in Mitchell Krugel, *Jordan: The Man, His Words, His Life.* New York: St. Martin's, 1994, p. 36.

136. Quoted in Krugel, *Jordan,* p. 33.

137. Krugel, *Jordan,* p. 33.

138. Herzog, *The Sports 100,* p. 77.

139. Quoted in Krugel, *Jordan,* p. 34.

140. Quoted in Krugel, *Jordan,* p. 73.

141. Quoted in Krugel, *Jordan,* p. 74.

142. Herzog, *The Sports 100,* p. 77.

143. Quoted in Herzog, *The Sports 100,* p. 77.

144. Quoted in Anderson, *The Story of Basketball,* p. 111.

145. Krugel, *Jordan,* pp. 49–50.

146. *CBS Sportsline.com,* "Michael Jordan Chat Transcript," March 22, 2001, http://www.sportsline.com.

147. Quoted in Bob Greene, *Rebound: The Odyssey of Michael Jordan.* New York: Viking, 1995, p. 35.

148. Quoted in Krugel, *Jordan,* p. 109.

149. Greene, *Rebound,* p. 17.

150. Quoted in Greene, *Rebound,* p. 17.

151. Quoted in Greene, *Rebound,* p. 9.

152. Quoted in Greene, *Rebound,* p. 275.

153. Greene, *Rebound,* p. 206.

154. Herzog, *The Sports 100,* p. 78.

155. Quoted in Herzog, *The Sports 100*, p. 79.

156. Herzog, *The Sports 100*, p. 79.

157. Quoted in Greene, *Rebound*, p. 220.

FOR FURTHER READING

Books

Nathan Aaseng, *Sports Great John Stockton*. Springfield, NJ: Enslow, 1995. A comprehensive biography of John Stockton.

Phil Berger, *Michael Jordan*. New York: Warner Juvenile, 1990. This well-written biography is part of the *Sports Illustrated for Kids* line and includes photographs and statistics.

Ron Frankel, *Wilt Chamberlain*. New York: Chelsea House, 1994. An in-depth look at the life and career of one of basketball's biggest stars.

Ted Gottfried, *Earvin "Magic" Johnson: Champion and Crusader.* New York: Franklin Watts, 2001. This biography looks at Magic Johnson's life, both on and off the court.

Keith Elliott Greenberg, *Magic Johnson: Champion with a Cause.* Minneapolis: Lerner, 1992. Focuses on Magic Johnson's career, as well as his work in raising AIDS awareness and helping black communities.

Robert Greenberger, *Wilt Chamberlain*. New York: Rosen Central, 2002. An easy-to-read biography of Wilt Chamberlain.

Timothy Jacobs, *100 Athletes Who Shaped Sports History*. San Francisco: Bluewood Books, 1994. This collection of capsule biographies includes entries on Wilt Chamberlain, Magic Johnson, Kareem Abdul-Jabbar, and Michael Jordan.

Michael Jordan, *For the Love of the Game*. New York: Crown, 1998. Michael Jordan talks about his career, his life, and his incredible rise to fame. Includes many excellent, full-color photos.

Martha Kreib, *Kareem Abdul-Jabbar*. New York: Rosen Central, 2002. An easy-to-read look at the life and career of Abdul-Jabbar.

Jacob Margolies, *Kareem Abdul-Jabbar*. New York: Franklin Watts, 1992. This biography covers the highlights of Abdul-Jabbar's playing career and personal life.

The Official NBA Encyclopedia, New York: Doubleday, 2000. This comprehensive reference book features player biographies, as well as information on the history of the NBA.

Jeff Savage, *Top 10 Basketball Point Guards*. Springfield, NJ: Enslow, 1997. Includes biographies of John Stockton and

Magic Johnson, focusing on their careers and how they played the game.

Robert Schankenberg, *Teammates: Karl Malone and John Stockton.* Brookfield, CT: Millbrook Press, 1998. Looks at the careers of these two players, focusing on how they work together to help their team.

Books

Kareem Abdul-Jabbar, *Giant Steps*. New York: Bantam Books, 1983. This autobiography describes Abdul-Jabbar's life, career, and activism.

Dave Anderson, *The Story of Basketball*. New York: William Morrow, 1988. A comprehensive look at basketball's first ninety-five years, written by a Pulitzer Prize–winning sportswriter.

Biography Today Sports Series. Detroit: Omnigraphics, 1996–2000. This series includes detailed biographies about many athletes, including Wilt Chamberlain, Kareem Abdul-Jabbar, and John Stockton.

Wilt Chamberlain, *A View from Above*. New York: Villard Books, 1991. An outspoken and lively autobiography touching on his experiences both on and off the basketball court.

———, *Wilt: Just Like Any Other 7-Foot Black Millionaire Who Lives Next Door*. New York: Macmillan, 1973. Wilt Chamberlain's first autobiography, written shortly after he retired from basketball.

Joe Garner, *And the Crowd Goes Wild*. Naperville, IL: Sourcebooks, 1999. This book and CD-ROM set includes many of the most exciting moments in sports, including Wilt Chamberlain's 100-point game.

———, *And the Fans Roared*. Naperville, IL: Sourcebooks, 2000. This follow-up to *And the Crowd Goes Wild* includes several exciting basketball moments in text and on CD-ROM.

Bob Greene, *Rebound: The Odyssey of Michael Jordan*. New York: Viking, 1995. A noted journalist follows Michael Jordan as he attempts a career in baseball.

Brad Herzog, *The Sports 100*. New York: Macmillan, 1995. Contains detailed biographies of one hundred great athletes and their influences on sports and society, including George Mikan, Michael Jordan, and Magic Johnson.

Earvin "Magic" Johnson, *My Life*. New York: Random House, 1992. Magic Johnson's autobiography, completed shortly after he disclosed he was HIV-positive.

Mitchell Krugel, *Jordan: The Man, His Words, His Life*. New York: St. Martin's, 1994. An in-depth look at Michael Jordan's years with the Chicago Bulls, featuring many quotes from the superstar player.

Michael Lewis, *To the Brink: Stockton, Malone, and the Utah Jazz's Climb to the Edge of Glory*. New York: Simon & Schuster, 1998. This book follows the Utah Jazz through the memorable season of 1997–1998 and describes the incredible teamwork of John Stockton and Karl Malone.

George Sullivan, *Great Lives: Sports*. New York: Charles Scribner's Sons, 1988. Profiles twenty-nine athletes from a variety of sports, including Wilt Chamberlain.

Periodicals

Kelli Anderson, "George Mikan," *Sports Illustrated*, August 22, 1994.

Ira Berkow, "Mikan Makes a Comeback," *New York Times*, March 26, 1997.

———, "Mikan Ruled an Era, and Changed the Rules," *New York Times*, March 11, 2001.

Ron Fimrite, "Big George," *Sports Illustrated*, November 6, 1989.

Richard Hoffer, "Welcome to the Club, Big Guy," *Sports Illustrated*, November 11, 1996.

Jack McCallum, "Pure Magic," *Reader's Digest*, May 2002.

Websites

CBS Sportsline.com (www.sportsline.com). Features the transcript of an online chat between Michael Jordan and his fans in March 2001.

Current Biography Excerpts: Basketball (www.hwwilson.com). Includes capsule biographies of basketball's most noted players.

Hoopman.com (www.hoopman.com). Includes fact sheets on players who have been elected to the Basketball Hall of Fame.

JazzHoops.com (http://jazzhoops.net). An article describing John Stockton's attitude and abilities.

Michael Jordan Biography (www.geocities.com). This fan site features a biography of Jordan.

NBA.com (www.nba.com). The official site of the National Basketball Association includes player profiles, photographs, statistics, and much more.

Sports.yahoo.com (www.sports.yahoo.com). This search engine can guide you to player profiles and stats on NBA players, past and present.

Sports Trivia (www.sports-trivia.net). Includes an overview of George Mikan's career, along with some insightful quotes.

The Ultimate John Stockton Page (www.geocities.com). A fan site that includes a short biography, statistics, career highlights, and quotes about John Stockton.

INDEX

National Basketball League
(NBL), 17
National Invitational
Tournament (NIT), 16

Olympics, 75–76, 83, 85

Pachter, Marc, 20
Peterson, Robert W., 14–15,
17
Philadelphia 76ers, 31
Philadelphia Warriors,
27–29
Pippen, Scottie, 84
Pistano, Cheryl, 48

racism, 25–26, 36, 56–57
records
set by Abdul-Jabbar, 49
set by Chamberlain, 29–31,
33
set by Jordan, 84, 90
Reinsdorf, Jerry, 86, 87
Riley, Pat, 49, 62
Rogers, David E., 66
Roller Hockey International, 21
segregation, 25
Shilts, Randy, 65

sky hook, 38, 49
Sloan, Jerry, 74
Smith, Dean, 82
Stabley, Fred, Jr., 58
Stern, David, 35
Stockton, John, 12, 69–78
abilities of, 73–74
All-Star games and, 76
childhood of, 69–71
college career of, 71–72
Olympics and, 72, 75–76
personal life of, 78
professional career of, 72–78
view of fame of, 77–78
Swift, E.M., 91

Tar Heels, 82
Taylor, Phil, 71, 77

Utah Jazz, 72–74

Walker, Darrell, 83
Washington Wizards, 90
Westhead, Paul, 61, 62
Williams, Gus, 71
women athletes, 33–34
Wooden, John, 41–42, 43
Woolridge, Orlando, 83

Picture Credits

Cover: center, lower left, © Bettmann/CORBIS; upper left, © Duomo/ CORBIS; upper right, Associated Press/AP; lower right, © Reuters NewMedia, Inc/CORBIS

Associated Press/World Wide Photo, 18, 24, 27, 30, 32, 41, 42, 47, 54, 63, 75, 77, 84, 87, 88, 90, 91

© AFP/CORBIS, 70, 72, 73

© Bettmann/CORBIS, 11, 14, 16, 19, 20, 37, 39, 45, 48, 56, 57, 60, 62, 65

© Reuters NewMedia/CORBIS, 67

© Getty Images, 28, 34, 81, 85

Library of Congress, 43

The Kobal Collection, 50

Yearbook.com, 23, 53, 80

About the Author

Joanne Mattern is the author of more than 125 nonfiction and fiction books for children, including two biographies for Lucent's People in the News series, *Tom Cruise* and *Celine Dion*. Her favorite subjects are animals and nature, but she has also written biographies of explorers and sports figures, an encyclopedia on U.S. immigration, classic novel retellings, and activity books. Ms. Mattern lives in New York State with her husband and two young daughters.